OUT
OF THE
CULTS
and INTO the
CHURCH

Understanding & Encouraging
Ex-Cultists

JANIS HUTCHINSON

kregel
RESOURCES

Grand Rapids, MI 49501

Out of the Cults and Into the Church by Janis Hutchinson.

Copyright © 1994 by Janis Hutchinson.

Published in 1994 by Kregel Resources, an imprint of Kregel Publications, P.O. Box 2607, Grand Rapids, MI 49501. Kregel Resources provides timely and relevant resources for Christian life and service. Your comments and suggestions are valued.

Cover Design: Tammy Johnson, FLAT RIVER GRAPHICS
Book Design: Alan G. Hartman

Library of Congress Cataloging-in-Publication Data
Hutchinson, Janis, 1931–
   Out of the cults and into the church: understanding & encouraging ex-cultists / Janis Hutchinson.
     p. cm.
   Includes bibliographical references.
   1. Church work with ex-cultists. 2. Ex-cultists—Pastoral counseling of. 3. Ex-cultists—Religious life.
I. Title.
BV4460.55.H88   1994   259'.08'69—dc20   94-11837
                                                     CIP
ISBN 0-8254-2885-8 (paperback)

2 3 4 5 Printing / Year 98 97 96 95

Printed in the United States of America

OUT OF THE CULTS
and INTO the CHURCH

Understanding & Encouraging Ex-Cultists

To my mother,
whose drive for spiritual truth above all else
directed and inspired me in my own quest;
to members of cults whom God will, in His own time,
bring out;
and
to those former cult members
who have already made the courageous move.

CONTENTS

Preface   9
Acknowledgments   15

1. No, You're Not Cracking Up: *Understanding
    the ex-cultist's trauma*   17
    How Can Christians Help?   31

2. Culture Shock: *When two worlds collide*   35
    How Can Christians Help?   46

3. Conflict of the Soul: *Understanding cult losses*   55
    How Can Christians Help?   70

4. No "Quick Fix": *Counseling with compassion*   77
    How Can Christians Help?   89

5. Loss of Roots, Story, and Identity: *Explaining the
    ex-cultist's disorientation*   95
    How Can Christians Help?   107

6. The Principles of Mass Movements: *How to combat
    the idea the cult was started by God*   113
    How Can Christians Help?   129

7. Ritual: *Examining the convert's loss of
    religious ceremony*   133
    How Can Christians Help?   144

8. Deadly Doctrines Tough to Divorce: *Why ex-cultists
    are reluctant to give up sacred stories*   151
    How Can Christians Help?   166

9. Exit from the Cult and Contact with a Pastor: *What
    to expect when it happens*   169
    How Can Christians Help?   182

10. The Precarious Transition Period: *A time of
    critical analysis and special needs*   187
    How Can Christians Help?   200

    Epilogue   207

    Appendix   213
    About the Author   221

PREFACE

problems
ex-culties.
ult → Christ
3 1372.

This book is not an exhaustive treatment of individual cults and their beliefs nor a book on how to witness. It is a book on the problems ex-cultists experience after their conversion to Christ, especially during the first three years.

During this difficult time, there are lingering problems that must be dealt with. If not addressed, the former cultist may begin church-hopping, drop out of the church, or worse yet, return to the cult.

To prevent these problems, the established Christian needs to maintain a special relationship with the new convert. The Christian's responsibility does not end with witnessing or bringing the new convert into the church. He or she must continue the task. And what is the task? Simply to continue.

Continue in non-judgmental caring so the ex-cultist will feel free to share his or her problems—especially after discovering that problems do not disappear at conversion. Continue by

9

helping the new convert move into every aspect of church life and seeing that he or she maintains that life until maturity.

It also involves continuing in the qualities Paul spoke of when he said, "Clothe yourselves with compassion, kindness, humility, gentleness and patience . . ."[1] When working with a former cultist, this is what it will take. These virtues will also help one gain deeper insight into the pain of what it means to be a former cultist and to respond to deeply felt needs.

One need not be hesitant about ministering to someone whose religious background differs so radically. Neither should one be reluctant because he or she has never been a cultist. Jesus, though never having been a mother, was able to speak with tender and profound sensitivity to the widow who lost her son. Although He only said two words, "Don't cry," He understood her loss and conveyed to her, "I understand—I'm here for you." Then He raised her son back to life.[2]

The Christian, though never having been a cultist, can also minister with spiritual sensitivity. He or she can also show compassion. What the new convert essentially needs to hear is, "Don't cry—I understand your loss—Jesus and I are here for you." Then like the widow's son, the former cultist can also be raised to new spiritual life.

The problems presented in this book are the more severe ones. Although some former cultists may suffer less than others, at least by understanding the extreme instances Christians will be equipped to handle all kinds of problems. By reading about their experiences one can enter their world, even if second-handedly. The Christian who is not a former cultist can use imaginative empathy which will help to acquire a fuller understanding of what one has not personally gone through.

In addition, because of the book's non-combative approach, it can also be given to new converts. Through it former cult members can gain needed insight into problems. It will

- assure them that what they are experiencing is normal,
- reassure them that they are not "cracking up," as some have expressed,
- give them confidence to persevere in spite of the problems,
- and offer hope by letting them know that others have succeeded in making it through the same difficulties.

This book covers "walk-away" ex-cultists—those who leave cults voluntarily and convert to Christ (as opposed to those who are forcibly kidnapped and deprogramed). Although some may claim there are "walk-away" ex-cultists who experience total peace with no lingering problems, I have yet to encounter any. I suspect this statement is the result of observing the superficial "front" of many newly-converted ex-cultists.

Some may not realize that a former cultist often hides problems. I say this not only because I did it, but because I have seen others give this appearance of peace and happiness. However, when given the opportunity to share with other ex-cultists, a different story is often revealed. Until I found this out, I thought I was the only one guilty of hiding my problems and had become quite good at it.

It should be noted, however, that this facade does not mean ex-cultists are pretending conversion to Christ. Neither are they intent on falsifying how much they love Jesus. What they are doing is falsifying a joyful behavior so as to hide depression over cult-related problems—problems that they believe Christians will criticize them for not overcoming sooner. Some believe this pretense will also help them gain faster acceptance.

Many of the ex-cultists with whom I came in contact were those sent to me by pastors who were bewildered as to how to help them. Others simply found their way to my doorstep. Some I contacted myself.

They met with me, not as a formally structured support group (although this technique is used in the book) but as friends who had something in common—problems. They honestly talked about their behavior and inner motives. They also shared private thoughts—thoughts they admitted they had not revealed to those working with them in their respective churches. Some visited a few times while others maintained contact for a longer period. Once they worked through their problems, however, they eventually went their separate ways. I had no more contact with them except for one ex-Mormon I've kept in touch with.

Only in a few places did I subdue the emotional remarks of typical converts. This is because ex-cultists, during their problematic stages, criticize the church and the pastor quite severely, expecting both to be exact substitutes for the cult.

New converts do not mean their remarks to be critical. It is their attempt to sort out their problems, come to grips with the difference between a cult and a church, restructure their lives into acceptable Christian patterns, and find new purpose and meaning. If the characters in the book come across as critical, please remember that they are being open and honest and are revealing their inner struggles.

The reader will notice that I quote frequently from secular research. This does not mean I necessarily agree or support the personal beliefs of some of the researchers. I quote authors whose particular insights lend clarification to the ex-cultist's mental condition, and I quote authors who have written about cults. Much of what they say has application to the ex-cultists described in this book. Their studies

- reveal why individuals join cults,
- indicate what they are looking for,
- show what it's like to leave a cult,
- interpret their losses,
- expose emotional problems,
- disclose the baggage they bring with them,
- confirm their longing to return to the cult,
- and explain their needs.

Many of these authors deal mainly with "officially" depro-gramed ex-cultists (they're easier to locate) instead of walk-aways. I found, however, that ex-cultists from both camps share common problems regardless of how they came out or what direction they take afterwards—entering society only or also entering a church.

Therefore, I agree with preacher and scholar John R. W. Stott in his book *Between Two Worlds* that it is necessary to construct bridges of communication between the Christian world and the modern world in order to "relate the one to the other with integrity and relevance."[3] He further adds that it is only by assuming the responsibility to delve into these "academic ivory towers" that we can help Christians "respond to it thoughtfully" and "be able to speak the divine Word to the human situation with any degree of sensitivity and accuracy."[4] Therefore, use of insights and principles from non-Christian sources should not be misconstrued as an endorsement of those authors' personal theology, conclusions, or opinions.

I admittedly lean heavily on ex-Mormon examples because they represent the majority of my ex-cultist contacts. In my research, I found their problems typical of those exiting other cults.

A special note to ex-Mormons and other former cult members who have converted to Christianity: even though you now know your former religion was unbiblical, I realize you still may cherish some cult memories. Therefore, you may be offended by the use of the word "cult." If I were writing this book in strictly academic terms, "sect" would be more correct. However, since "cult" is the term used by Christians at large, I have chosen to use it. However, no offense is intended, since the definition of a cult is a religious group which deviates doctrinally from the traditional norm.

This book will provide the reader with the tools necessary to understand and assist an ex-cultist during the difficult period after conversion. It will illustrate the traumatic problems a new convert must deal with and the adjustments he or she must make. It will analyze and clarify strange behavior and reveal private thoughts and concerns that are often withheld from Christian counselors. It will also present the misconceptions of Christians who believe an ex-cultist's problems occur *before* conversion, not *after.*

In this book I have focused on five characters—three ex-Mormons, one ex-Hare Krishna, and one ex-Moonie (Unification Church). While I have portrayed these characters as attending a formally structured weekly meeting, this was created solely for the purpose of combining their input into one compact unit so as to more easily relay information to the reader. A few other backdrops were also created for the sake of literary interest.

In addition, the use of either the masculine and feminine gender should be understood to include both, since there are no statistics which show the preponderance of one over the other when entering a cult. This was indicated in a telephone conversation with Dr. Michael D. Langone, Executive Director of the American Family Foundation, who stated that statistics derived from his own research and that of others do not conclusively indicate that one gender is more prone to join cults than another.[5] This statement, of course, would also apply to those leaving cults.

The lack of statistics is due to two major reasons. Former cultists are often unaware of the existence of counter-cult organizations and therefore make no contact with them (which could provide a statistical record). And many, not wishing to reveal their background, become "closet" ex-cultists.

Actual persons referred to in this book have given permission for inclusion of their remarks. While some of the dialogue is quoted verbatim, some is not. In the latter case, the essence of the conversation is accurately reflected. The characters presented in this book are composites, based upon other ex-cultists I have met, my own family members who came out of Mormonism, those interviewed by other authors, and my own experience. They are:

- Judy, an ex-Mormon
- Elizabeth, a former member of the Unification Church (ex-Moonie)
- Melanie, an ex-Mormon
- Myra, an ex-Mormon
- Richard, a former Hare Krishna

Since these characters are the author's creations, any resemblance to persons living or dead is purely coincidental. Unless otherwise noted, Bible quotations are from the *Holy Bible, New International Version*, copyright 1978 by the International Bible Society and used by permission of Zondervan Publishing House.

Preface Endnotes

1. Col. 3:12.
2. Luke 7:13–16.
3. John R.W. Stott, *Between Two Worlds: The Art of Preaching in the Twentieth Century* (Grand Rapids: Eerdmans, 1990), 338.
4. Ibid., 180, 189.
5. American Family Foundation, P.O. Box 2265, Bonita Springs, FL 33959.

ACKNOWLEDGMENTS

This work is the product of some years as my long-suffering but now relieved family can attest.

I am not only talking about the time it took for my manuscript to evolve from a master's thesis to its present form, but also the years I spent suffering through the transitional problems that inevitably face former cultists. I compared symptoms and problems with other ex-cultists, read everything I could lay my hands on about cults, tried to find answers and solutions as to why I was suffering so, and wondered when, if ever, I was going to come out of it and be a "normal" Christian.

Hopefully, this book will help established Christians to comprehend the spiritual and psychological post-conversion problems ex-cultists go through and also help former cultists understand what to expect during the recovery process.

I am grateful to my mother Ruth Stewart who, because of her ability and love for writing, critiqued parts of this book.

Special thanks go to my daughter, Debra, who checked over my manuscript, made suggestions, reminded me of events I had forgotten, and shared her heart-felt emotions in recalling her own problems following her conversion to Christianity.

There are no words that can express my gratitude to Pastors John and Wilena Cowen of Parowan, Utah, who worked with me after I left the Mormon Church. I believe God knew that no one else would have the love and patience to stick with me. Only they know what a difficult ex-Mormon convert I was. I have mentioned some of their methods in this book.

Special thanks go to Hope Coote, whose Christian Counseling class at International Bible College, San Antonio, Texas, not only helped me to psychologically analyze my own transitional problems but also directed me to useful information for this book.

I am grateful to those who labored with me through the first stages of my manuscript: Elaine Wright Colvin, Director of Writers Information Network; Connie Isakson; author Agnes Lawless; Brad Sargent of Exodus International for his help with my book proposal; Gloria Chisholm, who led the critique group I attended while working on my manuscript; and to my friend and professional consultant, Carol Christensen, for her invaluable insight and expertise during the last stages of my book.

I also wish to extend my thanks to the reference librarians at the Everett Public Library. Regardless of my many calls, they cheerfully provided the information I requested, thus saving me many trips.

Lastly, I am grateful to Dennis R. Hillman, my editor at Kregel Publications, who saw value in my book.

1

No, You're Not Cracking-Up

Understanding the ex-cultist's trauma

When Judy, an ex-Mormon, came to see me, she was emotionally distraught. After thirty years in the Mormon Church, she left and converted to Christ—but two years later she was still having problems. Frustrated and discouraged, she was willing to share her problems with another ex-cultist.

Sipping my tea, I studied this attractive woman in her mid-forties who had come to tell me her story. Intelligent and articulate, she held a master's degree—but she was also an ex-cultist.

We sat at a round, glass-topped table shaded by a lavender umbrella on the patio outside my Texas home. Lush foliage and beds of yellow and pink roses offered a serene setting. It was just what she needed.

"No one knows the anguish I'm going through trying to adjust to Christianity," Judy began. She set down her glass of iced tea, her hands slightly trembling.

"I feel like a horse is tied to my right brain and another to my left, and both are taking off in opposite directions. I'm in such a state of turmoil, I think I'm losing my mind! At night I pace the floor weeping, asking myself, *Why is this happening to me? Why can't I sleep? Am I going crazy?*

"I don't have any answers," she sighed. "The pastor and his wife don't either. They're surprised that I continue to have problems. They finally suggested I talk to you, hoping that perhaps as a former cultist yourself, you could relate to what I'm going through and know how to help me."

My heart went out to Judy. However, what she was going through was not unusual. I had seen it with other ex-cultists—the agony of sleepless nights; the conflict between harboring cherished beliefs and trying to erase cult indoctrination; the torment of wondering if it was a mistake to leave the cult; the hiding of problems from those working with them; and in addition, having to deal with the misconceptions of Christians who believe an ex-cultist's problems occur *before* conversion, not *after*. The former cultist suffers untold stress for months, even years, *after* leaving the cult. It is an intense, turbulent, and critical time.

Judy, somewhat more calm, continued her story by describing how she grew up loving Jesus in a Protestant denomination. But, after joining the Mormon Church when she was fourteen and spending most of her life as a Mormon, she began to grow hungry to hear more about Jesus. She stopped attending and began her search.

Finding a small Christian church in Utah, she asked if she could attend their Bible study.

"When I saw their happy faces," Judy said, "and listened to their exuberant singing about Jesus, I knew they had something I desperately needed. But, it was a shock when I found out they expected me to give up my beliefs!

"Letting go of thirty years of Mormon indoctrination created unbearable stress. At times, I became belligerent with those discipling me, especially when some believed I was demon-possessed. This only made me feel belittled and unacceptable."

"Didn't you have any close Christian friends who could help you?" I queried.

"Not really, except for Myra, another ex-Mormon. We met shortly after she came to Christ. I remember asking her if she was suffering as much I was. Her tearful response only reflected my own pain. Neither one of us could understand why we were so miserable.

"Desperate for answers, we drove six hours from southern Utah to Salt Lake City. We searched Christian bookstores, hoping to find a book which would explain what we were going through. Disappointed, we returned home."

Frustrated and lacking solutions, Judy admitted she nearly returned to the Mormon Church. But, having burned too many bridges behind her, she stayed in the Christian church—often miserable, always perplexed, satisfied with Jesus as her Savior but at the same time traumatized.

Judy nervously poured herself more iced tea. "Before my conversion," she explained, "I was energized by new friends witnessing to me. But afterwards, when their attentiveness slackened, it was different. I was really alone then.

"When two years passed and there was no relief from my problems, I determined to solve my own dilemma. I thought, *I'll switch to a different church*, believing that was the problem. That didn't materialize. Then I thought, *No, I'll go back to the Mormon Church*. I knew that was out of the question. Then I finally concluded, *I'll just quit church altogether!* Again, I couldn't do that either," she sighed. "There was no solution.

"I realize that I have to make it by myself, and so that's where I am now. But, I'm beginning to feel less and less like a part of the body of Christ. It's not the fault of the members; it's just that I have these overwhelming problems. How can I devote myself to Christ and the church when I have problems I can't explain?" At that point her voice broke.

I reached for a Kleenex and handed it to her. "Judy, it's natural to have confused feelings. Your predicament is not uncommon. Other ex-cultists feel the same way."

"But everyone is puzzled when they see me struggling with problems."

"The reason they're puzzled," I said, "is because they're misinformed and uneducated about the process.

"Christians have misconceptions. They assume a new convert made a clean break with the cult and is not clinging to former beliefs. They take for granted there will be no major after-effects and think it will be smooth sailing after conversion. 'God,' they say, 'will make the transition easy.' Lastly, they presume a former cultist will immediately adjust to church life."

Judy nodded knowingly.

"But, on the other hand, Judy, Christians are right to be puzzled. They ask, 'How can one love Jesus and still miss the cult leader? How can one believe Christianity is the truth, but question if leaving the cult was right? Why does one continue with agonized and sleepless nights when happy to be delivered from bondage? How is it possible to want cult indoctrination erased yet harbor cherished beliefs?'"

Judy sighed. "Yes, I know. It doesn't make much sense." Exhausted, she leaned back in her chair.

Studying Judy, I felt sorry for her. But I also knew the dilemma Christians face. Educated to believe that Bible doctrine and knowledge of cult beliefs alone equip them to deal with ex-cultists, they soon find themselves sorely inadequate. They wonder what more they can do than what they've already done. They feel helpless. Some throw up their hands and abandon the battle. Others withdraw personally but continue to pray. Some redouble their efforts, which only heaps guilt on the already struggling ex-cultist. Some generalize and say, "It's because he came out of a cult, or the cult demon hasn't left yet."

After I explained this to Judy, she questioningly searched my eyes.

"Is there such a thing as a cult demon?" she asked.

"Well, Judy, in my own mind, I don't think that's the answer to most ex-cultists' problems. However, most admit it's not difficult to arrive at such an answer.

"Here," I said, reaching for a magazine from the coffee table; "you might be interested to know what one author says about it.

"He reports that 'about 85 percent of therapists and clergy don't really know what happens to people in cults; therefore, they can't really help and may even misdiagnose former cult members. Often ex-cultists are [mistakenly] treated for schizo-phrenia.'"[1]

"Goodness," Judy exclaimed, "I hope no one decides that's what's wrong with me!"

"The point I'm making," I smiled, "is that if professionals are puzzled, it's only normal for Christians to be baffled also."

We talked for another hour about the transition process until Judy suddenly glanced at her watch. Reaching for her sweater, she rose from her chair and added one final remark. What she said didn't surprise me. I had heard it before—many times.

"My main frustration," she said, "is not only the ceaseless turmoil, but the fact that I don't know *why* it's happening. I've been wondering if I was cracking up."

"No, Judy, you're not 'cracking up.' Remember," I said, putting my arm around her, "there are valid reasons for your suffering. In time, understanding will come."

Judy and I walked down the gravel pathway leading from the patio. As we made our way through the trellised vines and red geraniums, she turned and said, "I'm so relieved to find another ex-Mormon. I wish I could have talked with you three years ago."

"Come again," I warmly invited. "I'm looking forward to our next visit."

"I am too," she smiled, as she waved a friendly good-bye.

As I watched her drive away, I thought, *It's too bad ex-cultists have such a rough time. Worse yet, not to understand why.*

Many have no idea what the underlying causes are for their upset. In a feeble way they can describe their symptoms, but that's all. Some researchers report that all ex-cultists can do is make such statements as "I never knew such bewilderment, pain, and feeling on the brink of insanity," or "I cried all the time."[2] The new convert, trying to understand the reason for his or her anguished state, often grasps at straws. This is what another ex-Mormon did.

"Something has to be wrong with the decision I made to leave the Mormon Church," Melanie exclaimed. "Otherwise, why am I so messed up? Maybe it's God telling me I made a mistake. This might make sense, because you know the saying, *If something is of God, one will feel peace—if not, it's of Satan.* Wouldn't it seem logical that my constant state of confusion since I converted means Christianity is wrong and Mormonism is right?"

With this kind of irrational thinking plus continual emotional behavior resulting from so many problems, it was no wonder pastors were sending their new converts to me. One of them was Elizabeth, a former member of the Unification Church founded by Korean-born Sun Myung Moon. As we sipped tea in bone china cups in my living room, the petite twenty-year-old described the dilemma of Christians who were trying to help her.

"I know what they're saying about me," she confided. "I have a close friend who tells me. They say: 'Why hasn't God eliminated her problems faster?' Some ask, 'Why is she still hanging on to that Moonie literature. She'd be okay if she'd just get her head on straight.' Others say, 'maybe she isn't really converted.' Some blame me and say, 'It's her own fault she's still having problems—she's just emotionally immature.'"

Elizabeth set down her cup and looked me in the eye. "You can't imagine how that makes me feel, especially when I'm trying so hard. I do love the Lord, even though I have problems I can't understand. Some feel I'm a lost cause—and maybe I am." Her voice caught. She put her hands over her face, and her shoulders shook with deep sobs.

I joined her on the sofa and put an arm around her. "Your feelings are perfectly normal considering what you've come out of, Elizabeth. Many people escaping cults have problems for years—even after their conversion to Christ."

"Really?" She dabbed at her eyes with a tissue.

"Of course. I did, too. And think about this: If you as a new convert can't figure out your problems, how can established Christians understand? They're strangers to this phenomenon. I'm sure the people working with you are only showing their concern."

"I suppose you're right." Elizabeth blew her nose and straightened up.

"I know so," I said. "I'll help you all I can. With the Lord's help, we'll conquer this together."

Elizabeth suddenly threw her arms around me. "I'm so glad to find someone who understands!" She left with a smile, promising to return.

There are many reasons why former cultists like Judy, Melanie, and Elizabeth are miserable. Their problems consist of more than just letting go of cult beliefs. Former cultists go through a death—not only the death of their previous cult structure but also their former self-image, identity, security, support system, and roots. It takes time to get over a death. New believers, therefore, cling to former doctrines, attitudes, and behaviors like beloved friends, refusing to let go.

This clinging causes myriads of problems that may persist from two to eight years. Researchers Flo Conway and Jim Siegelman say an ex-cultist may find himself "'floating' in and out of altered states," having "recurrent nightmares," and unable "to break mental rhythms of chanting [and] meditation." There are also memory loss, hallucinations, delusions, and suicidal tendencies.[3] Although Conway and Siegelman's study refers to professionally de-programmed ex-cultists, the same symptoms often plague walk-aways.

Adding further to the ex-cultist's trauma is what Dr. Margaret Singer of the University of California calls the "fish-bowl" effect. She describes the "constant watchfulness of family and friends, who are on the alert for any signs that the difficulties of real life will send the person back."[4] Although Dr. Singer's research also deals with kidnapped and professionally de-programmed ex-cultists, the fish-bowl effect is once again also experienced by walk-aways.

Christians guilty of this "staring" mean well; however, ex-cultists misinterpret their intent. It makes them feel "peculiar." When I met Richard, an ex-Hare Krishna, he described how this felt.

"I feel like an intruder trying to enter their world," he said. "Often I catch church members staring at me when they think I'm not looking—as if I'm some kind of oddity. Although I've attended their church for a year, they still make me feel like I'm in one sphere and they in another. Their expressions of love, though probably genuine, seem to me to be condescending—as though I'm some immature person who doesn't have any sense because I belonged to a cult. They're still watching for signs indicating I might go back. It's obvious I'm not one of them yet."

When an ex-cultist enters a Christian church, he feels different. Even though this feeling may only be in the mind of the new convert, to be different is such a traumatic experience that, desperate for acceptance, he feels pressured to put on a facade. He will do anything to escape feeling different, even if it means pretending.

Myra told me of the ploy she used to avoid being different among her new church friends.

"I wore myself out pretending to be a full-blown Christian," she said. "Of course, I *was* a Christian. It's just that I was still hung up on a few cult beliefs. Not doctrines, just beliefs—like having lived in a pre-mortal world. I also suffered from depression for reasons I couldn't identify.

"I wanted so much to be like them—not to be known as 'the Mormon' anymore. Even though I was converted to Christ and loved Jesus, I felt I had to convince them. So, I entered in and acted just like they did, testifying, singing hymns with gusto, smiling, even agreeing with them about how wicked the Mormon Church was.

"I spent a lot of time putting on a joyful countenance, then went home and cried, knowing all my actions were a farce. I still had problems! Even though I no longer believed in the cult, I still wasn't free of it. In fact, I missed it! But if I hadn't put on a front, they would have wondered why I wasn't over my problems. My depression would have showed—and Christians, from my observation, aren't supposed to get depressed."

Myra's facade doesn't mean all converts pretend; considering their many problems it would be safe to say that many do. Judy admitted she did the same. I asked her why she tried so hard.

"I guess, because I wanted acceptance," she replied. "But, I also tried harder because I was offended. Their words and actions indicated they thought I was some ex-cultist who didn't love God or know anything about Jesus. Albeit Mormon doctrine teaches a non-biblical Jesus, the Jesus I personally knew and loved while in the Mormon Church wasn't a 'different Jesus' like so many insist. Maybe it was my Protestant upbringing," she explained, "but, I adored the One in the Bible who died on the cross for my sins. After converting to Christianity and when saying my prayers, I didn't say, 'Dear Jesus,' hoping that some other deity by the name of Jesus would answer. I felt hurt. All I wanted was to be accepted as an equal."

This pretense, which new converts become quite good at, keeps established Christians from realizing that they are still suffering serious problems, that their desperate cover-up is dictated by their need for acceptance. New converts, determined to avoid any aspect of rejection, will do whatever it takes to be accepted.

Even three to four years later the need for acceptance and the shame of still having problems can make one continue the facade. Admittedly, this is what I did.

After moving to another state, I returned after two years and revisited my church. While chatting with the pastor's wife, I could tell she thought I was over my problems—but I wasn't.

She jokingly said to me, "You don't know how impossible you were! Sometimes I just threw up my hands in desperation, made a beeline for the bedroom, slid to my knees, and told the Lord I had no idea what to do with you. Since He was the one who started this work in you, it was His responsibility to see you through—I'd done all I could!"

I laughed along with her, letting her think my problems were indeed a thing of the past. But by so doing, I played a hypocritical role which only compounded my situation.

As problems persist, the new convert keeps them well camouflaged for fear of censure. This cannot help but have disastrous effects.

When I first met Melanie, the ex-Mormon, she told me that when she first knocked on the pastor's door, she burst into tears when she saw him. "I don't think I'm born again! Can you help me?"

But I could see that even with her desire to be "born again," she was still emotionally distraught, suffering the inevitable transition problems. Much of her distress, however, was because she did not share these problems with those working with her.

By suppressing emotions, her body suffered. One day when we were in her car, she pulled up her ankle-length skirt. Her legs were covered with ugly sores that had broken out as a result of her emotional state.

Physical afflictions, I discovered, are not uncommon during the rehabilitation period. Conway and Siegelman observed that disorders range from "extreme weight gain or loss; abnormal skin conditions such as rashes, eczema and acne; menstrual dysfunction in women," and, in addition, "one in five experienced some lasting health problem."[5]

When the troubled converts covers up anxieties, they only fester beneath the surface and contribute to a prolonged recovery. The whole experience is so difficult that some wonder if it's worth it.

"I just didn't realize," one former cultist said, "the personal trauma associated with leaving a cult. If I had known beforehand how difficult it would be and how long the turmoil would last—I don't think I would have left."

Surprisingly, Richard, the ex-Hare Krishna, echoed that remark. "I'm so worn out from the stress and anxiety," he said, "that I'm about ready to conclude that Christianity isn't worth what I'm going through. This doesn't mean I don't love Jesus, but a person can only take so much without help."

In addition, Judy described what she went through six months after her conversion. She told me how alarmed she became, believing she was having a nervous breakdown.

"Wracked with emotion," she said, "I remember running to the mirror to see if my face looked any different—I was surprised I still looked like me. Panic took hold as I convulsed under strange feelings I couldn't describe. Frightened—I felt like I was physically coming apart. Soon I became hysterical.

"*Thank goodness,* I thought, *the pastor's home is always open.* Amid a profusion of tears, I dialed his home number. 'I've got to come over right now. I don't know what's happening to me!' Slamming down the phone, I jumped in my car and was there in five minutes. The pastor and his wife began praying for me while I shook and cried. Gradually their soothing voices, speaking the Word of God, calmed me down."

Judy later told me that by hindsight she believed the breakdown was the consequence of the stress she was under for so long—hiding her problems, not wanting to give up beliefs, having one foot in Mormonism and one foot in Christianity.

"But," Judy added, "I suppose it was good I went through that horrible experience. Otherwise I would have been offended when I later overheard the pastor's wife say to someone, 'An ex-Mormon is a mental and emotional mess.'"

Melanie was also one of these "emotional messes," especially the Sunday morning she walked out in the middle of the sermon. I followed close behind, and we sat in her car.

"I think I'm losing my mind," she said with a sob. "What if Joseph Smith was *really* a prophet of God? If I continue with these Christians I might lose my 'exaltation.' I might even end up in 'outer darkness' and become a 'daughter of Perdition!' I can't sleep at night and it's driving me crazy! What shall I do?"

Melanie's distress was typical of other former cultists. Conway and Siegelman confirm that two-thirds of the ex-cultists they contacted experience "long-term emotional difficulties."[6]

Sitting in the car and listening to her, I was amazed. This was not the happy, out-going Melanie I was used to seeing in church. She, like many other ex-cultists, had acquired a proficiency at covering up problems.

Of course, much of the pain could be reduced if new believers talked about their anxieties with Christian counselors. But there are two reasons new converts may not share: fear of being judged incorrectly and, secondly, not wanting to appear different. Richard, the ex-Hare Krishna, told me why he would not admit his struggles.

"After my conversion to Christ," he began, "I knew if I said I was still having serious problems, my Christian friends would wonder why God wasn't blessing me. Besides, if I had, it would have blown my cover, revealing I still had a long way to go before becoming one of them. By pretending I had no problems, I'd appear more 'Christian'. But my charade only made me feel hollow and hypocritical."

"Well," I said, "since acceptance was your primary goal, maybe by sharing your problems you would have established the bond you were looking for."

Richard thought for a moment, then shook his head. "How could I relay something I didn't understand? I could have described my symptoms, but beyond that I was helpless. There were times when I actually thought I was cracking up and didn't even know why."

The inability to analyze one's own problems causes additional stress. Authors Irving Hexham and Karla Poewe agree. "Individuals who find themselves in states of emotional turbulence are rarely able to voice, and still less to analyze, their problems. This makes them susceptible to panic."[7]

As a result of these problems, the ex-cultist is difficult to work with. Myra, Judy's ex-Mormon friend, admitted how troublesome she was.

"I became obstinate, disputatious, and difficult," she said. "Even now, I sometimes defend the cult! When I give our pastor and his wife a trying time, I say to myself, *Myra, you're completely hopeless. You're not going to make it in this church!*

"When I become dogmatic and headstrong, I get angry with myself—especially when I know the pastor and his wife are only trying to help. *Much more of this,* I keep saying, *and I doubt I'll survive.* But I suppose those working with me probably wonder if *they'll* survive! I'm sure they must be disgusted with me. If they are, I think it's because they just expect too much too soon."

Another problematic area is reluctance to give up cult literature. "I know I'm supposed to give up Reverend Moon's book, *Divine Principle*," Elizabeth said, "but I can't give it up just like that!" she exclaimed. "Yet I can see from others' viewpoint why they feel I shouldn't claim to be a Christian and still keep the book on my shelf. Nevertheless, I just can't seem to let go of my cult books in spite of my sincere conversion. If my Christian friends knew this, they'd probably give up on me. This is what frightens me—for fear they'll decide I'm not progressing fast enough and turn their backs on me."

Sad to say, Elizabeth's fear is valid. Author and former Mormon Sandra Tanner confirms this:

> Many times Christians become really impatient for a Mormon to move faster, but each person has to mature at his own rate
> For instance, a person may accept Christ and still hang on to some remnants of Mormonism.[8] [My husband] Jerald and I . . . hung onto the *Book of Mormon* for two years after accepting Christ, and when some Christians who knew us at that point found this out, they more or less washed their hands of us . . .[9]

Established Christians, using Acts 19:19 as a basis, insist the new convert should burn all cult literature *immediately.* But it won't work if the cultist is not ready.

If this statement comes across as saying it is not important to burn cult literature, let me add this: when it is done, it effects a significant break. This action was very effective in my own experience; in fact, it produced quite a miraculous change for both me and my daughter. But the *timing* was right. If I had been forced to do it when I *first* entered the church, it would not have worked. In fact, it may well have had a reverse effect. The ex-cultist already knows Christians expect him to destroy his literature, so when the time is right, he will do it on his own. Since former cultists are often censured because they still hang on to cult literature, they feel forsaken and devastated beyond words. It only motivates the new convert toward one alternative—return to the cult!

But there are other reasons besides the above which contribute to the desire to go back. Melanie explained her reasons.

"It was my unreal expectations which nurtured my longing to go back," she began. "I just expected too much from my new church.

"I counted on the pastor to make the same extra-biblical claims as Mormon leaders. I anticipated the same opportunities for service. I looked for the same intensity of personal relationships and group bonding. I hoped for the same high idealism and sense of cause. I wanted the same kind of security!"

In the midst of problems like these, Stuart A. Wright says many remain confused for up to four and a half years over the decision they made to leave the cult.[10]

Unfortunately, no hard statistics are available on how long this plaguing doubt or desire to return will last. But according to personal interviews I've made, it appears to be from three to eight years.

One former cultist shockingly admitted that she did not overcome her longing for *twelve* years. However, she explained that her desire to return was not the result of continuing turmoil *per se.* While others went back as a means of seeking relief from their stress and disappointments, this was not her reason. She felt Christian churches were weak in fulfilling basic needs—and she knew the Mormon Church excelled in that area.

How long can one expect to have problems? In speaking with former cultists, I find that the length of time varies, but many admit three to seven years. For ex-Mormons, it may take three years just to let go of the *Book of Mormon.*

Conway and Siegelman's study reveals that up to *eight* years after leaving the cult, one in seven will experience disorientation and traumatic aftereffects.[11] In speaking with Utah pastors who regularly work with walk-away ex-Mormons, I found they also cite a period of three to eight years. One pastor said, "It normally takes months for an ex-cultist to become free of problems—years, if there is no help."

Another pastor said, "Some Christians just don't understand what's going on. They think their job is over in a few weeks."

When a cultist is brought to the altar, says the sinner's prayer, attends church every Sunday, and acts like other Christians, it doesn't mean he or she is free of problems. Conversion to Christ doesn't supernaturally and instantaneously undo old ways of thinking.

I wondered if there was any way the lengthy process could be shortened. Richard offered some ideas.

"Ex-cultists need someone who can give them answers. I wish someone could have explained two things: what was happening to me and how long my problems would last. Just to be told would have cut down on the time factor, not to mention my discouragement."

Elizabeth agreed. "I had no logical answers for why I was miserable. If someone had told me ahead of time what to expect, I could have anticipated problems, recognized them as normal, and bided my time till they passed. I kept saying to myself, 'When am I ever going to get the cult out of me and be a normal Christian? Why am I suffering so? If I just knew, I could cope better!'"

"How important is it then," I asked, "for Christians to become educated?"

"It would make all the difference in the world!" Richard quickly responded. "In the middle of being 'messed up,' I certainly didn't have the presence of mind to figure out what was at the root of my anxieties. No one will know how close I came to shaving my head and going back to Krishna! Former cultists have to rely on Christians to explain what's happening to them, or they'll go back to the cult."

Myra agreed. "I know from what I'm going through now," she said, "that there is no way I can fully devote myself to God or to my church until my problems are resolved. But the dilemma is, I can't resolve them because they first need to be identified and defined. I'm unable to do this, because I don't know what's happening. This is where established Christians can help."

Their observations were sound. Well-informed Christians can make a difference. But when cult doctrines have been skillfully implanted into one's belief system for years, it may take a long time. If no help is available, the former cultist will do one of three things: continue to suffer but stay in the church, drop out and become spiritually inactive, or return to the cult.

How Can Christians Help?

1. *Be perceptive.* Perceive the trauma associated with departure from a cult. Acquire a special sensitivity which recognizes that the cultist's first defecting step causes a severe crisis within him.

The sympathetic Christian can say to the new convert, "I realize you have given up everything you once held near and dear and you're going through a difficult trial. But I also recognize that God has led you here. He won't let you down now. Neither will I. I'm here for you, and we'll get through it together." Then minister with applicable Scriptures. The former cultist can then maintain spiritual equilibrium during the painful transition.

2. *Be polite.* Don't point out how terrible the cult is. The former cultist retains a kind of loyalty to the cult, even after conversion to Christ. If you offend, you may lose him or her.

3. *Be informed.* Become familiar with the new convert's concerns. Learn how to detect the cause of problems. Remember, ex-cultists do not understand them. They are only aware of the effects. They need someone to identify problems for them and tell *why* they are going through this ordeal. (The following chapters will provide this.)

4. *Be prayerful.* Ask God to give you the ability to recognize problems the new convert has so you can pray in specifics rather than in generalities. Then you can say, "Father, I believe

this is the problem she is going through. Help me to know what to do." Being explicit with the Lord will produce effective and often amazing answers.

5. *Be humble.* Don't assume the former cultist has no affinity for God. Ex-Mormon Judy insisted that neither her love for nor personal concept of Jesus changed when she converted to Christianity—only her doctrines.

6. *Be sympathetic.* Seriously consider the problems a former cultist must address. He or she must

- develop graciousness towards family and friends who do not understand one's personal crisis,
- struggle with an inability to identify one's own problems,
- acquire tolerance for those who belittle and condemn the new believer's former membership in the cult—with some insisting he or she has a demon,
- persevere in the face of emotional struggles,
- show bravery in stepping forth into a strange, new culture,
- and continue in the Christian walk when no one seems to understand, even other believers.

7. *Be reassuring.* The Bible tells us how to deal with traumatized people like the new convert: "Comfort, comfort my people, says your God. Speak tenderly to Jerusalem" (Isa. 40:1).

Explain to the ex-cultist that emotional turmoil is normal, considering the situation, that it takes a long time to give up old beliefs and it doesn't happen overnight.

Assure the new believer that you understand. In moments of agitation, persuade him or her that they are not "cracking up." Explain that certain stages are necessary for all converts from cults to work through. Affirm that as traumatic as these stages may be, they *will* pass, and the truth will eventually set them free.

8. *Be wise.* After you have become more informed, don't "dump" all your newly acquired knowledge on the new convert the minute the first problem evidences itself. Pray that God will give you "an instructed tongue, to know the word that sustains the weary" (Isa. 50:4). By allowing yourself to be guided by the Holy Spirit, you will know when the time is right to share your insights.

9. *Be available.* Don't leave the new believer to fend for himself. When he or she first makes an appearance in church, and even after conversion, they need a firm and dedicated Christian to stick with them. Be sure to tell them, "My home is open to you any time of the day or night." Sheila Garrigus, ex-Mormon, recalls how problems often became magnified in the dark. She "would wake up many nights in desperate fear," and was grateful she had an established Christian she could call on.[12]

When Christians can empathize, educate themselves on the former cultist's post-conversion problems, and act accordingly, the new convert will gain confidence, acquire stability, and move toward full maturity.

The following pages will identify the causes underlying the new convert's agitated and strange behavior. Although there are many causes, there is one that must be understood up front before any of the others. It alone provokes enough trauma to send the former cultist packing.

Chapter 1 Notes

1. William Kent Burtner, "Don't Be So Sure You Can Say No to a Cult," *U.S. Catholic* (April 1990): 23.
2. Flo Conway and Jim Siegelman, "Information Disease," *Science Digest* (January 1982): 88.
3. Conway and Siegelman, 88. See also Stuart A. Wright, *Leaving Cults: The Dynamics of Defection* (Washington D.C.: Society for the Scientific Study of Religion, 1987).
4. Dr. Margaret Singer, "Coming Out of the Cults," *Psychology Today* (January 1979): 80.
5. Conway & Siegelman, 88, 90.
6. Ibid., 90.
7. Irving Hexham and Karla Poewe, *Understanding Cults and New Religions* (Grand Rapids: Eerdmans, 1987), 108.
8. Latayne C. Scott, *Ex-Mormons: Why We Left* (Grand Rapids: Baker, 1990), 122.
9. Ibid., 114.
10. Wright, 91.
11. Conway and Siegelman, 90.
12. Scott, 119.

2

CULTURE SHOCK

When two worlds collide

The shock shattered me! It was like someone had crept up behind me and hit me full force with a baseball bat—I saw the pastor drinking coffee!"

As Myra, Judy's ex-Mormon friend, shared with me, my heart went out to her. This twenty-six-year-old young woman with auburn hair and blue eyes displayed the mixture of emotions I recognized so well—the anger, the pained, bewildered look, the wrenching struggle to keep back the tears.

Her emotional reaction was not unusual. Myra's two worlds had collided. She was going through religious culture shock, that violent conflict one encounters after leaving one religion and entering another—a painful, disabling, and threatening experience.

Like other former cultists, Myra had not let go of doctrines she believed were of divine origin. She still carried her cult baggage with her, coffee abstinence and all. She needed help; otherwise, she might slip back into the arms of the cult.

I had briefly met Myra before, but this was the first time I had been to her apartment. She ushered me into the front room, inviting me to sit on the couch near an open window. It was a balmy evening, and the slow rhythmic chorus of crickets offered a serene backdrop. However, this was not reflective of Myra's emotions. Shock and inability to cope with Christians drinking coffee had left her frantic.

"As a dedicated Latter-day Saint," Myra began, "I believed in the 'Word of Wisdom' and strictly lived it. No coffee, tea, alcohol, or tobacco—not even Coca Cola. My body was a temple for the Holy Spirit!

"When I saw the pastor drinking coffee," she continued, "I managed to cover up my upset—as usual. But questions shot through my mind: If the pastor is God's anointed leader in a church that is supposed to be more true than the cult, how can he violate his body? If he's in contact with God, then God should have given him a revelation about such things. Was Joseph Smith, who received a revelation on the subject of keeping one's body clean, more in tune with God than this pastor? Maybe Joseph Smith really *was* a prophet, and I've made a terrible mistake by leaving!

"You can't imagine the panic I felt," she said, her voice shaking. "I was a wreck the entire evening. I was nearly ready to chuck Christianity and go back to Mormonism."

Myra's behavior, similar to a traveler arriving in a foreign country, was not unusual. Encountering unexpected situations which conflict with one's perspectives, a traveler feels uncertain and anxious. He doesn't know how to respond. He experiences trauma and shock because he thinks all people are basically the same and should act as he does. When he discovers this is not true, he isn't merely surprised, he's threatened.[1] He feels different, unaccepted, fearful. In addition, communication is difficult if not impossible. He wants to return home! This is how Myra was feeling. I knew she also wanted to return "home."

"Just when I think I'm doing pretty good," she continued, "I come face to face with more upsets in the church. Like the disrespect of using the pronoun 'you' when praying, instead of 'thee' and 'thou.' And I just can't understand why the pastor doesn't claim extra-biblical revelation or why some preachers have to shout—it's so irreverent! And . . . passing the plate—I mean, how commercial can you get! Aren't Christians committed enough to volunteer their tithing without having to be asked?

"However," she quickly added, "I *am* convinced that Mormon doctrine is unbiblical—and I *have* decided I want to be in a church that goes by the Bible. But," she exclaimed, waving her arms in a frantic gesture, "I get upset over so many things! As a result, I sit in church looking at the Christians, and something inside me says, *Myra—you're different from these people—you don't belong here. Why don't you get up and leave?* Sometimes I do." With that, Myra got up and walked over to the window. She stood there for a few moments trying to control her emotions.

"Have you spoken with your pastor or someone else in the church about this?" I asked.

"Heavens, no!" she said, whirling around. "I can't explain myself to myself, let alone to them! Sometimes I don't even know why I'm upset. Besides, they'd think I was being critical." She paused. "It isn't actually criticism, you know. I don't know what it is." She dropped into her chair.

"Myra," I interrupted, "you're right where God wants you. You're going through a big adjustment right now. It's not easy to accept the fact that drinking coffee or other contradictions you're encountering may not be a sin. You came out of a church programmed to believe God literally dictates every standard and taboo. Now you're in a church that claims God doesn't do that—it's left up to the individual. You're not the first ex-cultist to experience culture shock, and you won't be the last."

"Culture shock?" she replied quizzically. "What's that got to do with church?"

Like many others, Myra had never thought of religion as a culture. But the Mormon Church, Jehovah's Witnesses, the Unification Church—even Christian churches—are all cultures. Each religion has its own world and unique ways of doing things—like a nation, tribe, or ethnic community. Each has its patterned ways of thinking and feeling—its shared symbols, meanings, values, ideas, standards, and bonds. Each establishes roles, forms self-images, transforms lifestyles and attitudes, and fosters certain behaviors and expectations in members. Christianity also produces these same elements. The major difference is, however, that it derives its cultural mores, mentality, values, and bonds not from self-appointed leaders but from God's revealed Word.

"Myra," I said, "considering the powerful influence a religion exerts, it's no wonder you're having a difficult time. At this stage, you're not able to stand outside of your former culture yet and see what an effect Mormonism had on you. One author put it very effectively. The effects of a culture on an individual are 'interwoven into a . . . complex fabric, woof and warp, color and pattern, without separation, stitched on the loom of each person's life.'"[2]

"So, what you're saying," Myra mused, "is that the cultural influence of a religion weaves the strands of our life into a pattern much like the pattern in a rug?"

"Yes," I replied, "and if you want to change that pattern, you have to undo every strand. The whole rug, of course, then falls apart."

"What do you mean?" Myra asked.

"I'm saying that when ex-cultists are confronted with new patterns which require undoing old ones, they are going to fall apart," I said. "It's as simple as that!"

"Simple?" stammered Myra. At that, she broke into uncontrollable sobs.

What Myra was going through would take time. Undoing old patterns and reweaving new ones is, as author Avery Dulles says, so difficult that it results in "mutual incomprehension, inability to communicate, frustration, and discouragement."[3]

Harold Bussell, in his book *By Hook or By Crook*, quotes authors James and Marcia Rudin who in *Prison or Paradise?* explain that "it can take years to overcome the fears and psychological damage incurred in a cultic group." Bussell agrees: "People often need professional help beyond what a pastor or church is able to give."[4]

After drying her eyes and blowing her nose, Myra asked, "Why do I react so violently over all this?"

"Myra, your reaction is perfectly normal. The sudden impact of seeing your pastor drink coffee was comparable to a head-on collision. Serious ruptures to parts of your mind were taking place. Let me explain.

"Everything we're culturally conditioned to believe and respond to is neatly arranged in 'filing cabinets' in our minds. Each drawer holds folders on various subjects. These folders contain our experiences, our beliefs, and our learned responses. For example, when we see dark clouds, our mind automatically pulls out a file on 'Weather.' It tells us to expect rain. Our response is to grab an umbrella.

"Every situation in life draws on these files," I said. "They constitute our picture of reality—the way we think things ought to be and the way we should respond.

"When you saw the pastor drinking coffee," I explained, "you went into shock over the difference between what your file on 'God's Health Laws' said you should expect and what you saw. You didn't know how to respond because you had no file folder that would validate his drinking coffee. Shocked by this contradiction, it was like the signals in your brain were short-circuiting. Naturally, you asked yourself, *If he were called of God, why isn't he keeping God's law?*"

"But, I even went home and cried about it," Myra said. "Imagine crying over something like that!"

"You were not only crying over the pastor drinking coffee; you were crying for other reasons too.

"Having your Mormon files neatly organized in your mind made you feel secure. Now your security was threatened. You felt as if someone had yanked all your efficiently arranged files and thrown them on the floor in a mess beyond rearranging. Your mind was at a complete loss—you had nothing from which to draw. Desperate to put everything back the way it was, you couldn't. You were crying because you felt powerless."

Myra nodded her head. "Go on," she said.

"In addition, all your beliefs about God and years of faithful abstinence were called into question—not to mention the authenticity of your new religion. In view of this disoriented state, you could react no differently than the way you did."

Myra dried her eyes and, though still visibly shaken, appeared pleased that her behavior had been so well defined.

Since she had prepared refreshments for my visit, she motioned me into the kitchen. Setting a plate of home-made chocolate chip cookies on the counter, she poured some lemonade into two glasses.

While we munched on cookies, she began sharing about the happy times and the disappointing times she had experienced in the Mormon church. She was still full of questions, so we pulled our chairs onto the patio and continued talking late into the night. We finally quit at two o'clock in the morning.

Myra, like many other former cultists, had two loads to carry. She was not only experiencing *religious* culture shock but also *societal* culture shock.

While *religious* culture shock is the difficulty one encounters after leaving one religion and entering another, *societal* culture shock occurs after a person first emerges from a cult and faces the shock of coping with reentry into society. This reentry alone is no easy task. One ex-Moonie, after being in the Unification Church for only three weeks, was seriously affected when he came out:

> Being out in the world again was a shock; a cultural shock in which I was unable to deal with reality. My isolation by the Church [the cult] had been so successful that everyday sights such as hamburger stands and televisions and even the people, looked foreign, of another world. I had been reduced to a dependent being! The Church had seen to it that my three weeks with them made me so vulnerable and so unable to cope with the real world, that I was compelled to stay with them.[5]

Considering all the theological, philosophical, and sociological unknowns in entering a new religion and that one suffers two kinds of culture shock, it is no wonder an ex-cultist has a difficult time. In addition, undoing what took years to build into one's belief system is no small task.

Late one afternoon I was surprised to receive a telephone call from ex-Mormon Melanie. She wanted to bring her mother to see me.

"She doesn't understand where I'm coming from," she said. "I try to explain this culture shock thing to her, but we always get into an argument."

"Why don't you come over after dinner?" I said.

They drove up to my house at 7:30 p.m. Typical of San

Antonio weather, they brought with them a sudden downpour of rain. Having no umbrellas, they made a desperate dash from their car to my front porch, splashing shoe-deep in water.

I ushered them into my warm kitchen and gave them towels for their hair. That broke the ice. We laughed amid introductions, joking as to why anyone in their right mind would continue living where rain always ended up resembling a flash flood. We then went into the living room with our cups of hot chocolate.

Joan, Melanie's mother, began the conversation. "Melanie says I'm like a bull in a china shop when I talk to her. I don't understand why she should be hurt when I tell her the truth. The Bible states that her cult beliefs are false, and anything false has to be of Satan. It's my responsibility as a Christian to tell her this. I try to help but only end up making her cry. It's affecting our relationship. In addition, she says I don't understand the 'culture shock' she claims she's going through. Melanie hasn't left the United States, so why is she saying this?"

I explained to Joan what I explained previously to Myra— that a person leaving a cult and entering a Christian church experiences the same kind of culture shock as a traveler entering a foreign country. To Melanie, Christianity is like a foreign country.

"Now, when a traveler," I said, "is unable to handle culture shock abroad, there are two options. One can withdraw and return home or else force oneself to become like the nationals.

"Melanie is choosing to become like the nationals— Christians. But, on the other hand, if she can't handle it, she has the other option. She can return to the culture she was once comfortable with—the Mormon Church.

"To really help your daughter, you need to be aware that she came out of something very different—not just doctrinally but a very different way of life. This calls for a special sensitivity."

"Go on," Joan said.

"Cultural sensitivity, first of all, requires one to set aside prejudice—not an easy task for some. Secondly, look into the heart of a cultist to see that she is not the depraved individual often pictured. She probably is not a seeker of darkness as so many believe. In fact, she more likely is a seeker of truth, albeit she erred in joining a cult.

"Many join because they are seeking truth, aspire to a more virtuous way of life, and hope for a closer experience with God. The reason they investigate a cult in the first place is to plumb the spiritual depths of all that is available.

"What leads them out, on the other hand, may be two reasons. The cult doesn't live up to its claims, or God is bringing them out based on what Christian theologians have come to call 'prevenient grace.'"[6]

"I'm sorry," Joan interrupted, "I don't understand that."

"Ex-cultists," I explained, "often say that before they joined a cult, they were praying that God would lead them to truth. Unfortunately, when they encounter a cult claiming to speak for God, they believe their prayers have been answered.

"The cult may satisfy them for a while, but sooner or later the unrest begins. This unrest," I explained, "is the divine urge of God drawing one or 'prevenient grace,' bringing him or her to the truth sought and prayed for in the beginning. Following these promptings out of the cult, he or she finally arrives where God intends."

I poured Joan more hot chocolate, then continued. "The Lord explains prevenient grace in Isaiah 42:16: 'I will lead the blind by ways they have not known, along unfamiliar paths I will guide them. . . . These are the things I will do; I will not forsake them'" (Isa. 42:16).

I suddenly glanced at the clock and noticed we had been talking for three hours. Walking over to the window, I closed it, then said over my shoulder, "I don't want to keep you too long, but I think we sort of got off the subject of culture shock."

"Explain again," Joan responded, "what you really mean by my being culturally sensitive."

"Sensitivity means, first of all, to recognize the Mormon Church as a culture. Next, to see how it has indoctrinated Melanie, affected her thinking, influenced her perspective of the world and others, and how it has established certain norms of doing things. If you can do this, it will give you the cultural sensitivity you need. You'll then understand why it's so difficult for her to give up old ways of behavior and thinking and why it takes time."

Joan, appearing more relaxed, exhibited a growing interest in the subject. While Joan was asking more questions, I glanced over at Melanie. The wall she had put up against her mother was starting to crumble. I felt it would be a profitable evening—and it was.

Early the next morning I was in the garden gathering roses when I heard the phone ring. I ran into the house. "Hello," I said, out of breath.

"This is Elizabeth." Her voice was hoarse from crying.

"What's wrong?"

"I don't think I'm going to make it in the church. I'm just not adjusting. I feel like throwing in the towel."

"Why do you say that?"

"I just heard about a missionary who went to India. The shock of being in a foreign country and trying to get used to new customs was so traumatic, he couldn't handle it. He ended up deserting his calling and returning home."

"Is that what you'd like to do, Elizabeth?" I set the basket of roses on the counter and scooted the kitchen stool closer to the phone.

"I think about it a lot," she admitted. "With all the wear and tear of undoing my beliefs and trying to make new adjustments, returning would sure be easier. If I were back in the cult, I could relax and feel happy and secure again. I'd know exactly how things are and what would be expected of me. And I'd have friends to talk to who would understand me. I guess I'm feeling like that missionary."

"Why don't you come on over?" I said.

"Great!" she responded quickly and hung up.

I hurriedly grabbed a vase for the roses and filled it with water. It wouldn't take long for her to arrive. Sitting on the porch, I waited. As I suspected, her car pulled up within ten minutes.

"I just don't know why I put myself through all this," Elizabeth started, with tears in her eyes. "What doesn't make sense is I think about going back but, at the same time, I love Jesus and want to stay with these happy Christians. Yet I'm not comfortable when I go to church because I think they're talking about me.

"I know I'm different. But I just don't know how to talk to them—and I know they don't understand me. We just don't speak the same language. I sure miss all my old friends."

"Well, Elizabeth, you're indeed in the same boat as that missionary. But, you certainly don't need to make the same decision he did."

"But what if someone just can't make the change?" Elizabeth asked.

"Well," I said, "those who can't make the change, as one author put it, become 'cultural casualties.'[7] But," I said, noting the alarm on her face, "you won't become one of them, Elizabeth. You're going to make it, not only because others have made it, but because I'm going to help you, and God promises to finish every work he starts."

I briefly reiterated to her, as I did to Melanie's mother, the realities of culture shock. What she was going through was nothing unique. World travelers went through it all the time.

"They too become frustrated and feel like aliens—especially when encountering the language barrier," I said.

"What do they do?" Elizabeth asked.

"They search for someone of their own kind—from their own country—someone who speaks their language. When they do, they form a fraternity. Let me give you an example.

"One summer, I found myself in a Mexicali hospital. There were no nurses who understood English—and my high school Spanish was failing miserably. I couldn't communicate, and sign language was frustrating. I faced a critical situation. Even if I did happen across a nurse who spoke a few words of English, I knew total understanding wasn't taking place because of the cultural difference.

"The few other Americans who found themselves patients in the hospital immediately began poking their heads into others' rooms, hoping to find someone—anyone—who spoke English. Those who weren't bedridden crowded into other patients' rooms, including mine, regardless of how sick we might be—just so they could communicate. Once they did, one would have thought we were all long lost buddies, even though we were strangers.

"It's not uncommon," I added, "for former cultists to feel the same way. They also feel like foreigners trying to communicate in a world they don't understand and, worse yet, where no one understands them."

"That sure is the way I feel," Elizabeth said. "I'm desperate to talk to someone else who understands. You're the only ex-cultist I know. Probably what I need is to find others who have become Christians. Can you put me in touch with any?"

That was when Myra, Elizabeth, Judy, Melanie, and Richard began meeting at my home. It was nothing formal or tightly structured—just friends meeting together who had something in common. They came with their pastors' blessings. It was a relief for each of them to find out they weren't alone.

The discussions were often moving and poignant. Other times they became quite analytical, as when they finally acknowledged they were indeed different from most Christians.

"After all, we have come out of a cult," Judy offered. "And long-time, established Christians do have different mind-sets and do speak another language."

"I think," Richard concluded, "that with all our crazy and weird problems and everything else considered, we're acting like normal ex-cultists."

"Yep," Judy grinned. "And I bet it'll be just a matter of time before we'll be calling ourselves normal Christians!"

Light-hearted discussions were frequent. Richard was always coming up with some "psychiatrist" joke. One he aimed at Elizabeth: "The psychiatrist said to the lady on the couch, 'You're not paranoid about Christians—what they're saying about you is really true!'"

Some get-togethers were spent sharing cult experiences, a procedure which cult researcher Susan Rothbaum confirms as beneficial. Reminiscing about one's cult days, she says, helps to say good-bye to the past, vent feelings about present problems, and look to the future.[8] All in all, the group gained strength in sharing their convictions about Christ and expressing hope for the future.

The next few days my thoughts were on Elizabeth, Richard, Judy, Myra, and Melanie. I could see progress, but it was slow. I knew that with their faith still in a quandary and emotions in a distraught state, family and friends were finding it difficult to show patience. I also thought about established Christians and their zeal in witnessing for Christ. I knew they had no idea how to handle an ex-cultist.

I recalled reading that in about a two-year period, forty thousand members left the Mormon church—many of whom would be entering Christian churches.[9] I also read about the two-year turnover of adolescents who join other cults, then leave when they reach adulthood. Seventy-eight percent immediately enter traditional churches.[10] I knew that if Christians were not prepared to help them, they would drift away or else return to their cults. I needed to come up with some suggestions on how to help.

I soon did. Derived from Philip Harris and Robert Moran's *Managing Cultural Differences,* and Craig Storti's book, *The Art of Crossing Cultures,* I adapted both to fit the ex-cultist.[11]

How Can Christians Help?

1. *Be informed.* Become knowledgeable with some kind of cross-cultural preparation.

What kind of preparation is needed? An excellent example is the training program described by Harris and Moran. Although designed for businessmen working in foreign countries, it also has application to Christians working with former cultists.[12]

The program stipulates what trainees need to learn in anticipation of their contact with another culture. They must become informed about

- behavioral patterns
- beliefs
- contemporary and historical figures
- family standards and structures
- food customs
- non-verbal forms of communication
- political systems
- power structures
- social structures
- religious holidays
- symbols
- motivational forces

Similarly, this same kind of advice is confirmed by Dr. Margaret Singer in her article, "Coming Out of the Cults." She admonishes those desiring to help cultists, especially therapists, that they learn all about a cult's program (not just the doctrines). If they don't, they will be "unable to open up discussions or even understand what is happening."[13]

When Christians are prepared like the trained businessmen, they will be more effective. For example, knowledge of food customs will give an idea of the shock a Hare Krishna or Mormon experiences the first time he sees a pastor drinking coffee. A Hare Krishna is taught that all food is spiritual, that eating is an act of worship. Coffee, as well as alcohol, tea, eggs, meat, and fish, are spiritually banned.[14] A Mormon believes God prohibits coffee, as well as caffeinated soft drinks, tea, and tobacco. Drinking coffee is a sin, comparable to breaking a commandment.

With this awareness, Christians can give the new believer an explanation about Christians' use of coffee before he or she actually encounters the situation. This will eliminate the severity of the shock.

2. *Notice similarities and differences between the new believer's cult and your own church (besides doctrines).* A Japanese industrialist made a vital and amazing observation about the differences between American and Japanese firms. He said: "Companies are 95% alike in their approaches and operations, but the 5% difference is what really matters."[15] Attention needs to be paid to the five percent. Those businessmen, anticipating contact with another culture but disregarding the five percent difference, experienced a high percentage of failure. In other words, without cross-cultural preparation, they had a 33–66 % failure rate. Contrast this, however, with those businessmen who took advantage of the training program. Educated to be sensitive to national customs, behavioral patterns, etc., they had only a 2 % failure rate![16]

Similarly, Christians may find ninety-five percent similarities between themselves and a Mormon because they both speak English, live in America, and possibly use the Bible. But, the five percent difference is what is crucial. It may mean the difference between failure and success.

3. *Be culturally sensitive.* A former cultist is convinced Christians have no idea what he or she is going through. Although Christians pray for an ex-cultist with the aim of being successful in winning the ex-cultist to Christ, it takes more than

just praying. If there is no understanding of the new convert's former culture and how leaving effects shock, rapport will not be established.

Lack of understanding will bring insensitivity. This can be seen when a well-meaning Christian insists the former cultist attend the Sunday School's class on "Cults." This class will not prove beneficial—it will have a negative result. The ex-cultist does not want to hear her cult's doctrines put down, even though she no longer believes them. Attacking a new convert's former faith is not effective.

Cultural sensitivity also allows one to understand the obstacles new converts are faced with. They must

- acquire group identity with new peers
- change their identity
- assess acceptable behavior
- break language and communication barriers
- cope with new cultural expectations
- determine norms
- give up old signs and symbols and embrace new ones
- master new customs and rituals

Lack of sensitivity may be one more factor that will push the new convert back into the arms of the cult.

How can one acquire cultural sensitivity? (1) By asking God to develop it; (2) by studying all aspects of a cult; and (3) by being willing to listen noncritically to the ex-cultist tell about her happy experiences in the cult. (Despite her reasons for leaving, she may still have fond memories she needs to talk about and work through.)

4. *Introduce the former cultist to a support group.* If one is not available, begin one. When a tourist experiences culture shock, especially if he intends to stay for some time in a new country, he looks for a support group to help him adjust.

An excellent example took place in India between 1857 and 1947. When the British army arrived in India, they went into severe culture shock. To survive their years of anticipated service, they created support groups or fraternities. However, they were so desperate they went to extremes. They created a miniature England! Author Craig Storti says they "chose to construct uncannily accurate replicas of Wilshire and Devon villages, complete with parade grounds, bandstands, . . . stone churches, picket fences, gravel walkways, even golf courses where feasible, clinging tenaciously to a lifestyle more passionately British, if the truth be told, than many of them had ever lived back home."[17]

Observer Charles Allen says that after coming in from the streets of India and stepping inside their home, "you were back in Cheltenham or Bath. . . . You went from bungalow to bungalow and you found the same sort of furniture, the same sort of dinner table set, the same kind of conversation."[18] It gave them necessary support while they adapted to the language and customs of India.

One, of course, doesn't expect ex-cultists to go to this extreme. But the experience above illustrates the problems when switching cultures and the desperate need to communicate with someone of like mind.

Similarly, the former cultist needs to find other individuals from his own country—those who speak his language. Through mutual support, the new convert can gradually let go of his past and adapt to his new culture.

5. *Suggest ways of handling culture shock.* Because of the shock former cultists receive from observing Christian customs and behavior which differ from their own, it often leads him or her to criticize, as well as to be offended. While it should go without saying that the new convert should rely upon God to help in those moments, the reality is that at the time of the upset he or she probably won't feel like praying. Therefore, a logical plan is also helpful.

First, explain to the former cultist what religious culture shock is. Tell him that one of the keys to handling it is *awareness,* then *analysis.* Craig Storti calls this process, "instinct override." It is the way travelers eliminate emotional stress and will also work for the new convert.[19]

Suggest that when he encounters a situation, the ex-cultist should train himself to become aware of his agitated feelings the *instant* they arise. Then he should analyze what is taking place. If he can shift into an analysis, his emotions will subside. This is because emotion and logic cannot occupy the same place at the same time.

Further, tell him: "At the moment of your reaction, say to yourself, 'I am making a judgment, but my judgment is based on my cult experience. I do not know enough about Christian customs or beliefs yet to have a legitimate grievance.'"

If the new convert can practice this instant analysis, a great deal of frustration will be neutralized. Here is a summary of the steps:

1. A cultural incident in the church occurs which is the primary *action*.
2. This causes a *reaction* (anger, fear, etc.).
3. He is then faced with *two options:* withdraw or become aware of his reaction and analyze it. By analyzing, emotions will subside.
4. He is then to *reflect* on the cause of his reaction.
5. Then his *reaction subsides.*
6. *Result:* The ex-cultist develops culturally appropriate expectations, and his sense of offense, anger, or hurt subsides.[20]

Eventually, the former cultist will see that his offended feelings are not a result of what Christians are doing to him or what they are doing against God, but because he is expecting them to think and respond with his same mentality.

Finally, ask him to set aside time at the end of each day to reflect on why he reacted a certain way. Have him write down the situation, his reaction, and analysis. Tell him you will discuss it with him later. When he recognizes that the cult conditioned him into having certain expectations and reflexes, he will see that Christians are neither sinning nor behaving incorrectly.

He then needs to repent, ask God's forgiveness for his criticism, and continue to ask for God's help to adjust to his new religious culture. His behavior will then be altered, and he can view Christian customs from a new perspective.

The above procedure was of great use in our home meetings. As Elizabeth attended our get-togethers, talked about her problems, and listened to others' advice and encouragement, emotional upheavals gradually subsided. It didn't happen overnight, but within the first year her reactions diminished, and her outlook became more positive:

"Although I talk about going back to the cult," she said, "I know it wouldn't work. I've got too much Christianity in me now. It's just nostalgia on my part—fantasizing about how it used to be. I know I left for good reasons. I also know I've come a long way, evidenced by the fact that I'm feeling more comfortable around Christians now. I believe I'll soon fit in more completely."

Myra, too, with suggestions from and the backing of the group, was able to pick up the disarray of file folders spread over the floor of her life. Gradually she replaced Mormon files with Christian files. She still abstains from coffee as a principle of good health but is not offended if others choose to drink it.

Melanie and her mother, Joan, became reconciled. At the close of that evening together, Melanie moved over to the couch and put her arm around her mother.

"Mom," she said, "even though God led me back into a Christian church, I can't undo years of indoctrination easily. I've been programmed to think and behave in certain ways. Criticism won't undo these ways any faster. It's going to take time."

Joan smiled sadly and began to cry. "I've really come down on you too hard. I'm so sorry."

Melanie and her mother embraced, and it was the beginning of a new relationship between them.

When a former cultist's world collides with the Christian world, trauma is inevitable. The conflict between beliefs, customs, and behaviors leaves the new believer bewildered and in shock. He or she experiences what Kurt Goldstein calls, "catastrophic anxiety . . . the most severe of all anxieties." Cultural anthropologists claim it produces "strong ego-destructive forces . . . ego impairment and weakening of the ability to function."[21] In view of this, it is no wonder a former cultist fears he or she will not make it.

Undoing beliefs is a slow process. But it will usually take care of itself as the new convert hears Christians declare over and over again what they do and don't believe and observes the church community in action.

As the established Christian makes him or herself accessible and teaches the new believer to rely on Christ, both the former and the latter establish a lifeline for the ex-cultist to cling to during the many crises. Having a Christian friend who is available and who has developed rapport through cultural sensitivity will result in a well adjusted, spiritually mature ex-cultist.

Although culture shock is the new believer's first major problem, there is another which, if not understood and allowed for, can extend the former cultist's depression and grief into an indefinite length of time.

Chapter 2 Notes

1. Craig Storti, *The Art of Crossing Cultures* (Yarmouth, ME: Intercultural Press, 1990), 58.

2. Charles C. Case, *Culture, the Human Plan: Essays in the Anthropological Interpretation of Human Behavior* (Washington: University Press of America, 1977), 49–50.

3. Avery Dulles, *Models of the Church* (Garden City, NY: Doubleday, 1974), 29.

4. Harold L. Bussell, *By Hook or By Crook* (New York: McCrackon Press, 1993), 206. Used with permission of the author.

5. Source unknown.

6. Henry Clarence Thiessen, *Lectures in Systematic Theology*, revised by Vernon D. Doerksen (Grand Rapids: Eerdmans, 1980), 106–107.

7. Storti, 32.

8. Susan Rothbaum, "Between Two Worlds: Issues of Separation and Identity After Leaving a Religious Community," in *Falling From the Faith: Causes and Consequences of Religious Apostasy,* ed. David G. Bromley (Newbury Park: Sage Publications, 1988), 217.

9. John Heinerman and Anson Shupe, *The Mormon Corporate Empire* (Boston: Beacon Press, 1985), 84. Figures for members voluntarily leaving and those who were excommunicated during 1981 and 1982.

10. Stuart Wright, *Leaving Cults: The Dynamics of Defection* (Washington: Society for the Scientific Study of Religion, Monograph series), 77.

11. Storti, 29, 58–65.

12. Philip R. Harris and Robert T. Moran, *Managing Cultural Differences,* 2d ed. (Houston: Gulf Publishing, 1987), 527–535.

13. Margaret Thaler Singer, "Coming Out of the Cults," *Psychology Today* (January 1979): 82.

14. John Butterworth, *Cults and New Faiths* (Elgin, Il: David C. Cook, 1981), 25.

15. Harris and Moran, x.
16. Ibid., 3.
17. Storti, 36.
18. Ibid., 36. Quoting from Charles Allen's *Plain Tales from the Raj.*
19. Ibid., 73.
20. Ibid., 29, 58–65.
21. Lawrence LeShan and Henry Margenau, *Einstein's Space and Van Gogh's Sky: Physical Reality and Beyond* (New York: Macmillan, 1982), 20.

3

CONFLICT OF THE SOUL

Understanding cult losses

With an explosion of emotion my daughter Linda blurted out, "It hurts to lose all those things! Christians need to understand how devastated you are! It's like a death!" Then she broke into tears.

"But, it's worse than a death!" she sobbed. "It's not like when just one person dies; it's like multiple deaths happening to you all at once! 'Things'—beliefs—securities—friends—start dying. If you lose ten things, you can't handle ten all at once. You're maxed out!"

Puzzled at her own outburst, she took a deep breath, grabbed a tissue, and added, "Gosh, I thought I was over this—because I know I would never go back."

Although I was startled, I knew Linda wouldn't go back either. Twelve years ago she left the Mormon Church and became a born-again Christian. She was offering these comments to show why Mormon losses are so calamitous and why there is the temptation for many to return.

Her reaction is not to suggest that all Christian ex-cultists will remain unhappy for twelve years. Rather, her recollections triggered the memory of what was once near and dear to her heart and how much it hurt.

And hurt it will. When a member exits a cult, she is engulfed by cult losses. When the one or two doubts that made her leave the cult are confirmed by zealous Christians, the questioning process is triggered even more deeply. The former cult member is then on her way to testing the validity of her beliefs, struggling with not wanting to let go, and sensing the loss in the procedure. Images and securities begin to topple, and the aftermath is one of pain, distress, torment, and bereavement.

Judy and I had just returned from shopping at the mall. Since it was close to noon, she invited me for lunch. While we sat at her kitchen table fixing tuna sandwiches, I told her about Linda's surprising outburst.

"After all these years," I said, "I never dreamed Linda's losses were still so poignant—especially since she's so happy and active in her church. She also admitted to secretly harboring cult beliefs for a long time."

Judy slowly nodded her head while reaching for the mayonnaise. "That doesn't surprise me," she said. "When I discovered I had to give up my beliefs, I decided to do the same thing. I was going to keep my favorite doctrines and just not let anyone know."

"So, at what point did you find it wouldn't work?" I asked.

Judy sighed. "Two long years—when I finally realized I couldn't hold two opposing doctrines at the same time and maintain my sanity. Not wanting to give them up, I tried to find another Christian church with beliefs like mine without my pastor knowing it. Of course, there was no such thing. I even investigated another cult."

"Have you overcome all your losses?" I sympathetically asked, remembering the difficult time she had.

"Not entirely," she said. "There are some losses I may never get over. Not because I still believe in Mormonism, but because I've found no substitutes in traditional churches that fulfill human needs like the cult did."

The phone rang, and the moment of sharing was lost. While Judy was gone, I began clearing up the dishes. There were so many losses after leaving a cult—too many for one person to bear at a time. I assumed I knew the losses Melanie, Myra, Elizabeth, and Richard still struggled with, but I wondered if they were suffering over others I knew nothing about?

When Judy returned, I said, "Wouldn't it be interesting to see how many losses our group could identify?"

She hesitated. "Yes—if they'll admit to them."

Thursday evening came and everyone arrived. After chatting amicably we went into the front room and settled into our favorite spots. When I told them my idea, their faces became somber.

"Do you think it's a good idea to talk about them?" Melanie asked. "It's taken a lot of effort to push them out of our minds and accept the fact that there are no Christian substitutes."

"Well, if we can list them, maybe later we can come up with some substitutes," I offered. "Let's try."

Judy helped by beginning the discussion. "My first sense of loss," she began, "was when I realized Christians had no extra-biblical revelation. I couldn't understand why God wasn't speaking to them! I was bewildered, wondering if I'd made a mistake in leaving the Mormon Church."

"I was perplexed too," Richard interrupted. "When the pastor tried to convince me Christianity was the real truth instead of Krishna, I thought that if that's so, why hasn't he received revelation about the cycles of creation, auras, or if we lived before this life . . ."

"Or," Judy laughed, "the eternal nature of matter, primordial substance, transmigration of particles, and spirit-matter."

Richard grinned. "Extra-biblical material is no longer a problem for me, Judy. But is it for you?"

Judy's expression changed as she shifted uncomfortably in her chair. "I admit I still miss it," she said. "For a long time I hung on to every word the pastor spoke, expecting him to expound on some new revelation. But he refused to deviate from the Bible. Even now I'm often bored—after all, I heard all the stories about Jesus when I was a kid.

"But don't misunderstand," Judy quickly added. "The need

to hear about Jesus is what excited me when I first converted. My mind was so worn out from my cult experience, especially my excommunication, that it was a relief to hear simple sermons. But gradually I became restless and craved more. I wanted to hear in-depth discussions like I was used to. But that was it—nothing new, nothing extraordinary, no insight into mysteries, no profound philosophies—just plain and simple 'Jesus'. It was difficult to come down to simple basics. Sometimes it still is."

Melanie, who had been quiet until now, looked at Judy. "We all know you like the deep intellectual stuff, Judy. But, to be honest, it's over my head. What I miss are the *Book of Mormon* stories." Her voice began to quiver and her eyes filled. Myra reached over and patted her hand. There was a long pause.

"My heroes were Nephi, Alma, and Moroni," she continued. "Those scriptures inspired me to live closer to God. I can't explain what the *Book of Mormon* did for me. It was really difficult to give it up." The others empathized, each recalling their own cult's scripture. I assured Melanie that we all understood.

Giving up cult scripture is stressful. It had been their source of inspiration. I quoted authors Irving Hexham and Karla Poewe who confirmed that where Christians claim that both the Bible and their lives take on new meaning after they are converted, cultists claim the same. Afterwards, however, without cult scripture, one's life then plunges into meaninglessness.[1] Everyone concurred.

"Well then," I said, scribbling on my note pad, "we now have number one: *loss of extra-biblical revelation.*"

"I think," Richard said, "that closely connected to that is the loss of supposed contact with God. This is what attracted me to the Krishna movement. I joined because the leader claimed he was directly contacting God."

"What happens," I asked, "when a convert thinks a leader has made contact?"

Judy, pulling herself out of her previous slump, quickly called upon her university studies: "When any religion," she began, "claims that God has revealed his true form to a leader, whether it's Lord Krishna revealing himself to the hero Arjuna, Christ supposedly appearing to Reverend Moon, spirit-guides appearing to 'I Am' leaders or, even in Christianity, the Lord revealing himself to Moses on Mt. Sinai, followers respond in a way that is more meaningful than if the revelation had never taken place."

"How's that?" Richard asked, obviously impressed.

"Faith is intensified," she answered. "One's prayer experience takes on stronger meaning, and one's relationship with God becomes more intimate. When a group, cult or otherwise, feels their leader is hearing from God, all spiritual systems are on high. Those who haven't experienced this have no concept of the degree of faith and devotion it can instill in followers.

"Imagine," she continued, as she leaned forward, "the difference it would make to Christians if they heard their pastors make this statement:

> And now, after the many testimonies which have been given of him, this is the testimony, last of all, which we give of him: that he lives! For we saw him, even on the right hand of God; and we heard the voice bearing record that he is the Only Begotten of the Father . . .[2] Then we saw Moses, Elijah . . .[3]

"What on earth is that from?" Elizabeth gasped.

Judy, who had memorized the passage years earlier, was quoting from *Doctrine and Covenants,* the book containing the Mormon Church's revelations.

"It's a precise illustration," she said, "not only of what every cult leader claims to have experienced, but what former cultists expect from pastors. I suppose most of you have gotten over this?" No one spoke.

Finally, Elizabeth blurted out, "How can you even ask? It hurts to lose something that was so meaningful! You all sit here talking so intellectually about it! It devastated me beyond belief. I miss it! The leader's revelations were my link with God! How can we expect to get over not having a leader we thought God was speaking through?" With that she broke into tears.

The others tried to comfort her, yet at the same time the look on their faces betrayed their same sense of loss. An uncomfortable lull settled in until Melanie cheerfully tried to change the subject.

"I was so used to Mormon leaders claiming contact with God," she began, "that I too had unreal expectations.

"Of course, I didn't quite come out point blank," she smiled, "and ask my pastor if he'd seen God lately. . . ." Everyone chuckled. "But," she continued, "I fished around by describing experiences Joseph Smith supposedly had when he saw God, hoping he'd say, 'I did too!'"

"What did your pastor say?" Elizabeth asked.

"Well, he must have known what was bothering me. Gently, but firmly, he replied, 'I have not seen God, and I have received no more information than what is in the Word of God. The Bible is all I need.'" Melanie gave a deep sigh. "It was the biggest disappointment I could ever have imagined."

"I guess I went through it too," Elizabeth said. "I judged my pastor by Reverend Moon. I wondered how I could rely upon what the pastor said about God if he wasn't claiming any direct revelation. After all," she continued, "Reverend Moon boasted of visitations by Jesus Christ."

"Yes," I interrupted. "And Moses David, of the Children of God, claimed contact with Joan of Arc; Eckankar members from Ascended Masters; Mark Prophet of the Church Universal and Triumphant acted as medium for the Archangel Michael; his wife, Claire, claims to be the incarnation of the Divine Mother; and Joseph Smith asserted he was taught by Peter, James, and John. They can't all be right."

"Well," Melanie said quietly, "I have to confess I'm still disappointed that pastors don't hear from God in a supernatural way—like having a vision, being transported to heaven, or seeing an angel. When the only information the pastor has about God is secondhand—from a printed page in the Bible, it makes me feel they're not 'chosen.'"

"But," Richard quickly added, "since learning about the 'still small voice' of the Holy Spirit, I believe that's the same as hearing from God!"

The others nodded in agreement—some more slowly than others. Elizabeth and Melanie just heaved a big sigh.

On my yellow notepad beneath *loss of extra-biblical revelation* I wrote: *cult leader's supernatural contact with God.*

These two losses automatically triggered the next: *loss of a divinely called leader.* I then shared with them why my daughter Linda particularly missed this loss.

"She believed her Mormon Bishop had been divinely called. As a result, he could select her for jobs in the Ward by direct revelation. After she left and found out that Christian procedure is to volunteer, her words to me were: 'To feel God isn't calling you directly is a real bummer.'" Everyone smiled.

"Fortunately," I continued, "Linda had a wise pastor. He watched for positions he could 'call' her to so she wouldn't have to volunteer. She was real impressed with that, especially because he called her to the music team. That's her love.

"However," I added, "pastors are indeed divinely led in their ministry. But, it isn't quite the same as what a former cultist expects."

Melanie interrupted. "Every time I used to see the President of the Mormon Church, I always fantasized that perhaps that very day, he visited with God."

"Yes, we all understand what you felt. Individuals are intensely attracted to a leader who claims to be divinely led. But the problem is that often God and the leader become fused in a believer's mind. Love for God, then, ends up as love for the leader with no distinct line between them. It's hard to let go of that kind of 'love.'

"This explains why it's so difficult for a cultist to renounce his leader. Logic plays no part—it's a matter of the heart. According to a study by Janet Jacobs at the University of Colorado, emotional bonds to a cult leader are always the last to go."[4]

"Well, then, that explains why," Elizabeth said, "I so fiercely defended Reverend Moon after I left. I didn't want to hear the truth about his indiscretions in Korea nor hear biblical arguments why he couldn't possibly be the Messiah. It was pure and simple. I loved him!"

"Don't feel badly, Elizabeth," I said. "After leaving a cult, feelings of love for a leader take a long time to diminish. To this day, I haven't relinquished my respect and admiration for the late David O. McKay, past president of the Mormon Church. Fortunately the pastor who worked with me had enough grace not to attack Mormon leaders. Because of this I was at least able, in time, to abandon the idea of McKay as 'Prophet, Seer, and Revelator.'"

"Well, one thing is certain," Richard began, "love or not, our leaders gave us solid direction. Whenever we had questions, there was no hesitation. They gave absolute answers. Hey," he suddenly exclaimed, looking quite pleased with himself, "I guess that's our next loss—*the loss of absolute answers!*"

As I scribbled it on my list, I said, "That's good, Richard. Dress standards, health habits, and moral guidelines, all the way to world problems are authoritatively answered by cults. How do you feel churches measure up?"

Richard was surprisingly emphatic. "I feel churches should address today's concerns! Should you become an activist in community and world issues? Can you smoke or drink? Churches should say something about it!"

Myra quickly spoke up. "When I first asked Christians if I could smoke, they said 'It's up to you.' It sorta made me feel at loose ends. When I was a Mormon, however, I knew exactly what the rules were. I could proudly say, 'I don't smoke because I'm a Mormon.' But now that I'm a Christian, I get confused because I find no such rules. No one will give me any absolutes in this respect."

"What is it we want then?" I asked. "A printed list of do's and don'ts, dictating every aspect of our life?"

"Is that so wrong?" Judy asked. "Everybody needs guidelines, even to white lines painted down the middle of a highway."

"Well," I said, "If our pastors gave such a list, would we be back in bondage again? Would our so-called worthiness be at stake if we didn't abide by everything on that list?

"Laws," I explained, "have no power to do anything for us. Remember that's what Paul said to the Christians at Galatia who thought that Christianity could only work if coupled with the Mosaic law. Isn't that what you're trying to do—incorporate both cult legalism and Christianity? Paul said, 'It is for *freedom* that Christ has set us free. Stand firm, then, and do not let yourselves be burdened again by a yoke of slavery' (Gal 5:1). Doesn't Christian maturity indicate we live according to our understanding of Christ and the dictates of our own Holy Spirit-led conscience? Could that be the exhilarating challenge to our new faith?"

"But," Myra interrupted, "I'm not asking for a list of *cult* rules.

I want a list of *Christian* rules, based on the Bible, so I'll know I'm really doing what God expects of me."

I glanced hopefully at the rest, but much to my surprise everyone concluded that while they understood what I was saying, for new ex-cultists such a list should be composed. They all decided to search the Bible and come up with a list and present it at our next meeting.

I could only hope that as they came to understand more fully the role of faith and grace in Christian growth, they would see the futility of such a list.

So far, we had named five losses:

- loss of extra-biblical revelation
- loss of a divinely called leader
- loss of absolute answers
- loss of a leader's supernatural contact with God
- loss of being called to positions of service by revelation

Like a word-association game, one loss called up another. The next was *loss of sacred myths.*

Richard and Judy—in fact all of them—admitted how they revered the marvelous stories surrounding their leader's calling. These divine visitations, myths in themselves, were supposedly initiated by Christ, an angel, or some departed spirit of historical notoriety. In addition, they claimed to receive heavenly knowledge unavailable to outsiders.

"A cult has a lot of sacred stories," I said. "How did believing these myths make you feel?"

Melanie ventured an answer. "Well, believing the Mormon pre-existence myth—that I left my heavenly home and was sent to earth—gave me a sense of identity and roots. I knew who I was and where I came from. I had a heavenly father and mother to whom one day I'd return. I had a specific mission in coming to earth. My goal was to accomplish what they expected of me and to return to them. After I was told pre-existence was false, I felt there was no reason for my being here."

"That's sort of the way I felt," Richard said. "In Krishna, I believed the myth that said I could change the world through chanting. But after I left, I had nothing to tune into any longer. I just walked around and didn't know who I was any-more."

They all admitted having serious problems with this loss. I could see that myths not only established roots and identity, but satisfied their basic need for answers, significance, and purpose. Giving them up hurled them into the chaos of opposites—doubts, insignificance, and ambiguity.

"Maybe this is pride," Myra interjected, "or maybe it was just excitement—but the doctrinal myths that provided detail about heaven gave me a feeling of being among God's elite. I knew what kind of reward I could expect in the hereafter and what level of heaven I'd attain. But in Christianity there's no clear-cut picture of heaven—just a vague, 'we'll be with Jesus.' With my cult's three degrees of heaven, it was really something to shoot for! . . . If it were only true," she sighed.

"Myra," I said, "I know this loss is particularly devastating to you. Ex-Mormons suddenly see their dream of becoming a god or goddess over future worlds destroyed. 'If they're not going to be a god, what are they going to be?' An ex-Mormon must *be* something! To lose a goal like that makes life seem purposeless. How can one go from something to nothing? It's quite a height to drop from until you reach an understanding of your position in Christ." Myra smiled a weak smile as I hastily scribbled down *loss of myths.*

The next loss wasn't difficult to name: *loss of friends and community ties.* This was still painful for them.

"It's bad enough to go through excommunication," said Myra, trying to hold back the tears, "but to be rejected by friends is terrible. Only one expressed sympathy to me—the rest wouldn't risk contact with me for fear of being reported to the Bishop.

"The humiliating part," she continued, "is that once I was excommunicated, I was considered in the 'devil's territory.' Members were afraid any contact with me would suck them in too. One friend met me on the street and glared at me with a look which shouted *traitor.* It was like he wanted to cry but, at the same time, wanted to hit me. To say I wasn't hurt would be a lie. I stayed at home a lot, feeling very alone in my silent house where the phone never rang anymore. I still cry some-times, wondering if it was worth it all. But," she quickly added, "of course I know it is. I know Christianity is the truth."

My heart went out to Myra and the others. Enduring excommunication and losing the regard of others provokes a sense of loss that is impossible to describe. It's one of the strongest motivations to return to the cult. It's also why Christian fellowship is crucial.

Everyone broke for refreshments, deciding to cover one more loss before calling it a night. They agreed to meet the following week with more, if any, plus their list of biblical guidelines for new converts.

Crowding around the kitchen table, we greedily piled our plates with olives, chips, stuffed celery, chicken salad, plus tempting and fattening desserts. Elizabeth smiled at me from across the table as she eagerly plunged her fork into a piece of whip cream-covered carrot cake. Her look seemed to say, *I can overcome these losses,* but I knew Elizabeth had a long road ahead of her.

We gathered in the front room again, ready for our last loss. After writing *loss of friends and community ties* on my notepad, we came up with the next: *loss of the only true church.*

"I really believed I belonged to the *only* true church God sanctioned," Elizabeth began. "When I first read *Divine Principle* and was convinced Christ actually appeared to Reverend Moon—that his church was the grand preparation for himself as the Second Coming Messiah, I was so excited!" The rest identified with her.

The divesting of this particular conviction proved to be one of the more problematic losses they had to deal with. They further admitted they came into a Christian church anticipating *it* to claim the "only true church" status—and believed it was a valid expectation. More confusion resulted when they learned of doctrinal differences among the denominations. How could *any* of them claim to be the true church and not believe the same?

After being firmly convinced that their cult had special favor with God, each agreed it was hard to admit they had been wrong—it was embarrassing to have been so sure. "We did so much boasting!" they said, recalling their enthusiastic witnessing. "We *knew* beyond a shadow of a doubt that our organization was started by God!"

Leaving the cult proved to be not only a disappointment but also a crushing humiliation. They felt it only confirmed to Christians their spiritual immaturity and inability to discern truth.

"Well," I concluded, "you have just added two more to our list. In addition to *loss of the only true church,* we now have the *loss of believing one is right.*"

"I just thought of one more," Judy said, "but I don't know what to call it. It has to do with the crazy picture some Christians have of cultists.

"I read about a psychiatrist who was motivated to write a professional paper because he wanted to know, 'What kind of nutty people get into these crazy groups?'[5] Since the author had a degree, I assumed he knew better and was just trying to be humorous—but he wasn't. Then I encountered this same predisposition while attending Bible college.

"As a former cultist on campus, I was often asked to share my story. I didn't mind being a curiosity because it gave me some degree of self-image. But after speaking in Chapel one morning, I noticed a fellow student making his way toward the professor who taught the cults class. Feeling he was going to comment about my testimony, I made my way over just in time to hear him say: 'I just don't understand it, in all other respects she appears to be intelligent.'

"The student's inference was, of course, that I was stupid for having belonged to a cult, and that my appearance of intelligence in other areas must be misleading. Until then, I assumed that as an individual I was his equal. I thought, *How could I have rubbed shoulders with this classmate for so long, and he not know the real me?* I was shocked and hurt. Hadn't any of these students recognized me as someone normal? I hadn't acquired intelligence only since becoming a Christian! I felt inferior and debased. Although logic told me my former cult membership didn't warrant this kind of assessment, my emotions overrode my logic, and I was devastated."

"Remember, Judy," I interrupted, "most Christians have never encountered ex-cultists before. But on our list we'll put *loss of respect.*"

Melanie brought some iced tea from the kitchen, and the remainder of the time was spent relating experiences.

As I sat back and listened to them, I realized how much they were going through and how much their losses hurt. Some openly cried while they shared. Linda's statement that losses were like "multiple deaths" was certainly appropriate. Glancing at my list, I thought of the popular consensus that a person is unable to handle more than three losses in a year. *Pity former cultists,* I thought, *not only three, but they must contend with twelve or more—and all at once! No wonder they feel like they're cracking up!*

After singing a song followed by many tears and hugs, the group said goodbye, promising to return next week.

I began clearing up the dishes, wishing Linda had been here. I was glad she was happy in her church, singing and playing the piano for God. I was also grateful her pastor had wisely "called" her to the music team instead of waiting for her to volunteer.

There was a sudden knock, and Linda opened the door and rushed in. "Sorry I didn't make it," she said, collapsing on the couch. "Music practice lasted later than usual."

I gave her a run down of the evening's events and showed her the list of losses.

"Well," she said, studying my notes, "there's one you left out."

"Oh?" I sat down across from her.

"Gosh, Mom," she exclaimed, "how could you forget the loss of self-esteem we both went through!"

Then I remembered. The Mormon Church rated personal significance very high—Adam's sin had no application to us because basically we were good. Self-esteem had risen to spectacular heights—but when we entered a Christian church, it plummeted to the very depths.

"Remember," Linda began, "how the pastor taught we had no merit or righteousness except to be described as 'filthy rags'? (Isa. 64:6). That we were sinners with a 'depraved nature'? And 'wretches' as in the song, 'Amazing Grace'?

"Yes," I mused. "I remember how depressed we were the Sunday we first heard that song. We certainly weren't prepared for the line which said, 'that saved a *wretch* like me.'"

I leaned back, recalling how stunned Linda and I had been that morning and how we fought against it. *We weren't degraded wretches—God loved us and as His creations we were worth something!* After the song, the preacher began speaking on the "worm" concept from Psalm 22:6. That did absolutely nothing for us, considering we already felt unacceptable as "ex-cultists."

After that morning at church, all Linda and I could think about was the appalling word "wretch." It wasn't offense we felt but severe depression and confusion. We felt we were no good and doubted our own value in God's sight. Any self-esteem we had was ripped right out of us. Linda was the first to talk about it when we arrived home that day.

"You know, Mom," she said, "whenever I've felt God's love, I've never sensed anything condescending about it. But, on the other hand, these Christians are supposed to be right, you know. Maybe we're wrong feeling like this. Maybe we really are worth nothing."

We spent a gloomy week honestly struggling to readjust our thinking and envision ourselves as "filthy rags." But every aspect of our being cried out against such a concept.

Linda's voice jarred me back to the present. "Mom, maybe it was hard on us because it was such a long drop from godhood. After all, what kind of image could Christianity possibly offer in place of that? When you've already been to the top of the ladder, then what? Where to from there?"

"There's only one way to go," I said, "and that's *down*."

We thought of other ex-cultists who enjoyed high esteem in their cult. They too found self-images crumbling. I knew this kind of letdown was, as Dr. Singer notes, one of the more serious problems ex-cultists have to face.[6]

"Well, we can thank James Dobson for helping us get over it," Linda smiled, reminding me of his book, *Hide or Seek*. "Remember him telling about meeting the elderly lady who spent all those years as a missionary? How she questioned his emphasis on personal self-esteem and felt God wanted her to think of herself as no better than a worm?"

I got up and walked over to the bookcase. "Here it is," I said, pulling it from the shelf. I turned to the dog-eared page and began reading aloud.

> This fragile missionary (and thousands of other Christians) had been taught that she was worthless. But that teaching did not come from the Scriptures. Jesus did not leave His throne in heaven to die for the "worms" of the world. His sac-

rifice was intended for that little woman, and for me and all of His followers, whom He is not embarrassed to call brothers. What a concept! If Jesus is now my brother, then that puts me in the family of God, and guarantees that I will outlive the universe itself. And that, friends, is what I call genuine self-esteem![7]

Linda and I smiled at each other. We knew now, that as a creation of God, we weren't "wretches" or "worms." How grateful we were to find other Christians who had this same outlook.

Linda had to leave, so I walked her to her car. Once back in the house, I picked up my list of losses. I had these thirteen:

- loss of extra-biblical revelation
- loss of a leader's supernatural contact with God
- loss of a divinely called leader
- loss of friends and community ties
- loss of believing one is right
- loss of belonging to the "only true church"
- loss of absolute answers
- loss of sacred myths
- loss of elite status
- loss of respect
- loss of being called to positions by revelation
- loss of goals
- loss of self-esteem

I thought about the evening's meeting. Everyone had done so well to list their losses. But I knew a deeper level of their emotions had been more repressed than expressed. Yes, they were still suffering, and I recalled the statement by authors McManus and Cooper:

> It is almost impossible for anyone who has not "been there," to comprehend the tremendous loss suffered by ex-cultists who have left behind them a package-deal life, full of love, support, and absolute answers—all structured around a purpose and goals. In its place sits a gaping void.[8]

And, such a void, I thought. Heavenly rewards obliterated, status quashed, community ties gone, friendships sacrificed, cherished myths given up, deeply-rooted beliefs forsaken. With no more prophet/leader they become directionless, purposeless, and believe they are no longer useful. Reduced to nothing, they undergo one psychological crisis after another. Their whole world comes crashing down around them.

Former cultists, says Dr. Eileen Barker, "find themselves . . . disillusioned and experiencing feelings of increased helplessness and hopelessness."[9] Phillip, an ex-cultist, as reported by McManus and Cooper, said, "I felt I could never get excited about living again. . . . I felt apathetic, drained of enthusiasm."[10]

It is no wonder, I thought, *that some spend up to eight years in a traumatic state of hopeless and inextricable confusion.*

Our little group was no different. Unable to handle their losses at first, they held tightly to whatever would maintain their link with the cult.

Richard clung to the *Bhagavad-Gita* and continued to wear his cloth bag and prayer beads around his neck. He also persisted in chanting in private. Elizabeth kept her vial of "holy salt" insisting it could still purify her life. Melanie refused to part with her *Book of Mormon*. Myra continued wearing temple garments for a full year. And Judy clung to her Mormon reference books.

In addition, they would occasionally revert back and defend cult doctrines. Richard would insist Jesus was not God but a pure devotee of Krishna visiting from another planet. Elizabeth argued that Jesus never redeemed the human race spiritually. Judy believed God was a resurrected man from a previous world, Melanie maintained she came from a pre-mortal world, and Myra thought Joseph Smith might be a prophet after all. Talk about discouraging! But, on the other hand, I knew that in time and with perseverance on my part, these ideas would dissipate.

How Can Christians Help?

1. *Recognize the ex-cultist's condition.* Acknowledge to the new convert that cult losses are distressing and that it will take time. Assure him it is normal to miss what had once been so meaningful to him.

2. *Inform her of the replacement method.* Tell her there are Christian substitutes for most of her losses. She can, for

example, replace cult myths with Bible stories. Challenge her to do this.

Ask the convert to take her favorite cult story and draw out important principles. For example, the *Book of Mormon's* story of King Benjamin portrays the principle of service to others. She can then be guided to Jesus' story of the Good Samaritan and others.

When the convert says cult scriptures inspired her, find comparable Scriptures in the Bible that are geared to producing the same motivation for the spiritual life.

3. *Establish a safe atmosphere.* Provide the former cultist with a non-judgmental environment, and he will feel freer to share the aspects of the cult that touched him the most. The Christian can then be made more aware of what substitutes the former cultist needs.

4. *Know what to expect.* The use of substitutes will not totally obliterate all memory of cult losses. This is an impossibility, as they are part of the former cultist's history. Tell the new convert however, that they will eventually fade and cease to cause grief.

5. *Define the pastor's role.* If the former cultist is troubled because her pastor does not receive the same kind of revelations or make the same extravagant claims as the cult leader, explain what "kind" of revelation is most helpful and needed.

A pastor's job is to care for his flock, not to "tickle the ears" of his followers. Ask the new convert what difference it makes to a flock to have a pastor proclaim the pre-existence of man or claim he can see auras? How does this help members solve life's problems, become better Christians, or draw closer to God? When one of the pastor's flock is hurting, this has no value at all. Explain that the greatest revelation in one's life is the fruit of the Spirit (love, joy, peace, etc.).

6. *Do not be offended.* If the convert indicates that sermons are too simple, it doesn't hurt to relay to him that you recognize his intellect. Tell the new believer the simplicity of Christian sermons will take getting used to. Do not take offense at the statement that sermons are boring. Keep in mind that cults often teach sub-

jects that are on a university level. However, point out that Jesus always kept His sermons simple. You might also suggest theology books for him to read, if he is past the salvation basics.

7. *Explain to the former cultist why he or she is having difficulty giving up the cult.* Tell the new convert that the reason she cannot let go of cult beliefs is *not* because God is telling her the cult is right, but for other very human reasons. There is love for what is held near and dear to one's heart. There is also fear of stepping into the unknown. These two factors always make one cling to the familiar.

8. *Help the new convert work out his problems by being a good listener.* Be willing to listen to the former cultist tell of the good times in the cult, as well as the bad, and resist the tendency to criticize.

The following are a few examples of how Myra, Judy, and Melanie's problems were resolved. However, lest the following sounds like all that was needed was logic and a few substitutes, and presto—they immediately overcame their losses—*not so.* Each went through frantic episodes of defensive arguing, crying, and sometimes anger before relinquishing their beliefs and accepting substitutes. There were also late hours and sleepless nights. But gradually success came.

Melanie gave up her *Book of Mormon* heroes after being shown how to transfer her affections to Old and New Testament heroes who exemplified similar spiritual traits. It was, however, also necessary to have her verbally denounce cult writings and rid her house of cult literature. This was not easy for her. This is also something I believe should not be done too soon (see chapter 9).

Myra and the others gradually gave up their myths when they were shown stories in the Bible containing similar themes which produced the same motivation for the spiritual life.

Their expectation that a Christian church should claim the "only true church" status, plus their confusion over churches teaching different doctrines, was worked out by presenting the concept of a "one true *spiritual* church," separate from denominationalism.

Judy's preoccupation with extra-biblical revelation gave her serious problems for a long while. Believing the Mormon idea that the Bible is not dependable because of translation errors, she felt many truths about heaven were lost and should be restored by modern revelation.

However, she finally accepted the Bible's completeness and sufficiency when shown that the ancient Isaiah text found among the Dead Sea Scrolls contained no major differences between it and the King James version. This launched her into a new conviction that the Bible had been divinely preserved—that there was no need for additional revelation.

The group eventually brought their "list" of Biblical guidelines to our meeting. They had laboriously enumerated New Testament admonitions: manage one's household correctly (1 Tim. 3:15); practice hospitality without grumbling (1 Pet. 4:9); bear one another's burdens (Gal. 6:2); and in Ephesians 4 and 5, don't tell falsehoods, be patient; don't become angry or curse; avoid dishonesty, bitterness, evil talk, slander, and impurity. They also listed an elaborate version of the Beatitudes, the Ten Commandments, and the Old Testament civil law. I was overwhelmed with their zeal to do everything right before God. However, as the discussion ensued, the presence of the Lord became evident as new insights began to develop.

"I wonder," Myra hesitatingly pondered, "if we want this list because we still have a fear mentality from the cult—because we believed for so long that if we didn't live up to the rules we would incur disapproval?

"While working on my list," she continued, "I came across Romans 8:15 that says we haven't received a spirit that makes us a slave again to fear. In addition, it doesn't say we're supposed to be controlled by a list, but our minds are supposed to be 'controlled by the Spirit.' Jesus never said the Spirit was a list, but a teacher. Doesn't that mean that His Spirit will automatically lead us into good works as well as keep us from doing bad works?"

Challenged, everyone tore into Romans and began an exegesis which would have intimidated the best of scholars. Finally Melanie said, "Verse one seems to suggest that if we slip and make an honest mistake, we're certainly not going to incur disapproval or go to hell. It says, 'There is now no condemnation for those who are in Christ Jesus, because through Christ Jesus the law of the Spirit of life set me free from the law of sin and death.'"

"When you think about it," Judy observed, "the Spirit-led life really boils down to one of choices. If my body is a temple and I understand that alcohol is bad for it, the Spirit is going to tell me not to defile it. If Jesus taught that what we look at enters our heart, then the Spirit will help me make wise choices about what to read and watch. If I know that some action will hurt my brother or make him stumble, then if Christ is in me and I'm in Him, as He says in John 14 and 15, then the Holy Spirit will teach me how to handle a sensitive situation."

As the evening came to an end, the group concluded that while the Bible does teach ethics and that it was wise to be knowledgeable about them, they felt a formal list had no place in their lives. They felt God wanted them to avoid legalism—because, they gasped, what if they missed listing some Biblical rule! They concluded that by turning their attention to the dictates of the Holy Spirit, they would be automatically led to observe biblical ethics and standards—plus, they would be more apt to develop spiritual maturity. Despite my earlier concerns, their exercise on the subject proved beneficial after all.

The process of resolution for all of them was heart-wrenching to watch. But the group came through because of three factors: (1) God, who starts a work of faith, always finishes it (Phil. 1:6); (2) they had a strong Christian working with them who relied upon promptings and wisdom from the Holy Spirit; and (3) each one in the group, though he or she had problems and missed the cult, believed Christianity was the truth.

The personal emotional reactions which accompanied their losses were difficult to deal with. I soon learned that each of their individual losses was coupled with intense grief. I gradually understood that both loss and grief are always consociates in the process—they go hand-in-hand. The next chapter will aid in understanding this association. It will also reveal why losses are comparable to the death of a loved one.

Chapter 3 Notes

1. Irving Hexham and Karla Poewe, *Understanding Cults and New Religions* (Grand Rapids: Eerdmans Pub. Co., 1987), 12–13.
2. *The Doctrine and Covenants of the Church of Jesus Christ of Latter-day*

Saints (Salt Lake City: The Church of Jesus Christ of Latter-day Saints, 1957), Section 76:22–24.

3. Ibid., Section 110.

4. Janet Jacobs, "Deconversion from Religious Movements: An Analysis of Charismatic Bonding and Spiritual Commitment," *Journal for the Scientific Study of Religion*, 1987, 26 (3): 306.

5. James T. Richardson, "Conversion, Brainwashing and Deprogramming," *The Center Magazine* (March-April 1982): 22.

6. Margaret Singer, "Coming Out of the Cults," *Psychology Today* (January 1979): 82.

7. James Dobson, *Hide or Seek* (Old Tappan, N.J.: Fleming H. Revell Co., 1979), 184.

8. Una McManus and John C. Cooper, *Dealing With Destructive Cults* (Grand Rapids: Zondervan, 1984), 77. Used by permission of the authors.

9. Eileen Barker, "Defection from the Unification Church: Some Statistics and Distinctions," in *Falling From the Faith: Causes and Consequences of Religious Apostasy*, ed. David G. Bromley (Newbury Park, CA: Sage Publications, 1988), 176.

10. McManus and Cooper, 75.

4

NO "QUICK FIX"

Counseling with compassion

He's been killed! A car accident!" Linda shouted over the phone.

The day started out lazy and sunny. I was relaxing on the patio lounge listening to the overhead drone of an airplane when the phone and Linda's voice shattered my thoughts.

"He's dead!" I heard Linda's frantic cry on the other end.

"Who's dead, Linda, who?" I panicked.

"It's Crinkle!" Her voice broke, and she began to sob.

I relaxed, sensing momentary relief. Crinkle was the family dog. But that didn't lessen the pain I knew Linda was feeling.

Part labrador and German shepherd, we brought Crinkle home as a pup thirteen years ago. He acquired his name from the fact that, unlike other dogs with straight whiskers, his grew in "crinkled." We all loved him. He had grown up with our family and eventually went to live with Linda when she left home.

We held the funeral in Linda's backyard. It was complete with pallbearers, flowers, music, a short sermon, and a ritual composed mostly by Linda's seven-year-old daughter Kimberly. Death, whether of pet or person, is a difficult shock to deal with. But the grief, the weeping, the farewells, and friends relaying sympathy helped us work through our loss. We were fortunate that society had established a custom for venting grief—even for pets. It effected the necessary "goodbyes" so crucial for our recovery. Without it, our mourning could have extended into a lengthy psychosis.

But there is another kind of death where no funeral, burial, or farewell is allowed. One which friends are incapable of understanding and so cannot offer sympathy. The grief is just as traumatic and the bereavement just as severe as when losing a loved one. It happens to thousands of former cultists every year—it is the death of their cult.

Swiftly slashed from one's life, this sudden and unforeseen loss effects a critical sense of tragedy. The former cultist, after years of physical and emotional attachment, is severed from a community which claimed to be his family—he is rejected by a leader who claimed to love him as only a father could. He grieves because the cult was tied to his own needs so deeply.

Hurled into a state of bereavement, he suffers the death of his identity, security, roots, self-image, basic needs, cult leader as father/mother, friendships, community, goals, causes, and many other essentials—all in one fell swoop. Ex-members lose "in a single stroke," notes Susan Rothbaum, "everything that has structured their lives and defined their personal identities, from mundane routines to the meaning of life."[1]

To recover, the ex-cultist must somehow bury the cult, acknowledge its death, grieve, and say farewell. But no such ritualistic opportunities are available for him. No ceremony, no burial, no final goodbye, no emotional relief through open expression of loss. More importantly, there are no friends able to offer the kind of compassion that comes from real understanding.

Christians may be sympathetic to a degree. Some may even be knowledgeable about the five stages of loss and grief. But they believe these stages apply only to someone mourning the loss of a relative or close friend. Therefore, they assume the former cultist has nothing to grieve over. They are unaware that losing one's cult and everything associated with it evokes the same distressful emotions as a death. It is as if Christians expect a former cultist to bypass all the stages of grief and experience nothing.

The ex-cultist, on the other hand, knows nothing about loss and grief stages—he is only aware of problems he cannot explain. Desperate for acceptance, he pretends to suffer nothing. If, by chance, he happens to be knowledgeable about the loss and grief syndrome, he strives to appear as if he has successfully passed through all stages or gone through none.

The new convert's stifled feelings prolong symptoms of nervousness, panic, insomnia, crying, nightmares, hallucinations, and flashbacks. Physiological ailments are also common as Ann Kaiser Stearns notes in *Living Through Personal Crisis*. "Not only through tears do we cry out pangs of grief [but] our bodies have a dozen ways of weeping with us."[2] The former cultist's facade is so complete Christians are oblivious to his true condition.

When Judy visited me in Texas, she recounted her distressing but puzzling behavior. She arrived one hot afternoon just as I was coming around the corner of the house dragging two huge plastic bags.

"Hi!" I called out. I gave the bags an extra swing onto the edge of the porch and sagged down in the shade on the front steps. "Cleaning out my basement," I said, wiping my forehead with my sleeve.

"Guess I came at a bad time," Judy laughed.

We sat for a few minutes while I cooled off. She told me of her new job as a legal secretary, a book she was reading, and other activities she was involved in. No one would have suspected she was going through anything.

"Grab the other bag, will you?" I said. "We'll go inside. I'm about ready for a cold glass of lemonade. How about you?" Judy nodded and smiled.

The front room looked like a cyclone had hit. Bags, boxes, lids, and twine were strung from one end to the other.

"Just step over everything and make your way to the kitchen," I laughed. "Drop the bag anywhere."

After placing a few ice cubes into glasses and filling them with lemonade, I motioned toward the patio. We each pulled a chair into the shade and sat down. It wasn't long before Judy started sharing.

"I just don't understand," she began. "Right after I left the Mormon Church and was having sessions with my pastor, we had nice, informative visits. I was very polite, amiable—so was he. He never spoke directly against Mormon leaders, and when he threw in Scriptures that invalidated Mormonism, I still enjoyed our exchange of thoughts. But then I started having insomnia at night.

"Have you ever had that uneasy feeling," Judy said, "that you were worried about something, but didn't know what? Well, that's the way I felt," she said. "I tossed and turned all night, but couldn't put my finger on what was gnawing at me. During the day, however, I was fine. I was happy attending church on a regular basis and was attracted to the joy everyone exhibited. I knew I wanted to be part of their church.

"Now, a year after my baptism, it's a totally different story. When I talk to the pastor, it's all I can do to keep a civil tongue in my head."

"What makes you this way?" I asked.

"The pastor might quote a Scripture like 1 John 4:12, *No one has ever seen God.* I'll contradict him and start arguing about Joseph Smith's vision and throw in Amos 3:7 for good measure—*Surely the Sovereign Lord does nothing without revealing his plan to his servants the prophets.* And," she gestured with her arms, "I don't even believe in Smith's claim anymore! I then insist that if God is in charge of His church, He ought to produce a modern-day prophet. Or, maybe he'll quote Jeremiah 1:5, *Before I formed you in the womb I knew you . . .*, and I'll hotly insist it means pre-existence not foreknowledge.

"Sometimes I lose my temper! I go home and it eats at me until I'm miserable. The crazy thing is," she quickly added, "I accept the Bible. I'm excited about what Christianity holds for me. It makes no sense why I'm antagonistic and defensive of Mormonism.

"As I see it," she continued, "my feelings are chronologically in reverse. Logic says I should have reacted defensively when I *first* investigated Christianity and was closer to my Mormon experience. But, I'm more troubled now and reacting more unfavorably than I was then. Can you figure that out?"

Her voice trembled as she poured herself more lemonade. Leaning back she pressed the cold glass to her forehead and waited for an answer.

I felt sorry for Judy, but I knew exactly what was happening. She was in the early stages of two well-known grief syndromes set forth in *Loss and Grief* by George L. Engel,[3] and *Death and Dying* by Elisabeth Kubler-Ross.[4]

The first syndrome of loss and grief contains five stages. It describes the process an individual goes through in resolving the loss of someone or something other than himself. Similarly, Judy had lost something other than herself—her cult. It had died and "passed away" from her individual life space.

The second syndrome of *Death and Dying* also has five stages. It applies to the individual who is told he or she is dying and must face the reality that life is over. In like manner, a former cultist also feels his life is over. He senses instinctive needs within him dying—needs crucial for the survival of "self" but which were filled in the cult. Judy, like most ex-cultists, was suffering *both* syndromes.

Combining these two syndromes, I renamed the progressive stages as I knew they applied to former cultists.

1. Shock and denial
2. Protest and anger
3. Despair and final grief with possible continuing effects of:
   a. Delayed grief
   b. Inhibited grief
   c. Intellectualized grief
   d. Prolonged mourning
4. Voidness and resolving the loss (sense of emptiness and increased dependence upon others)
5. Acceptance and adjustment (This acceptance is not to be mistaken for a happy stage. Although the pain is gone and the struggle is over, it means one accepts the finality of the break with the cult and looks to the future.)

Judy opened her eyes. "Well? Any answers?"

"Since you like analysis so well, Judy, I'll do my best.

"To begin with, your withdrawal from the cult, that is, the sudden absence of it from your life, affected you like a death— much as someone who loses a loved one. When your relationship with the Mormon Church was suddenly cut off, even though you caused it to happen, you went into a stage called shock and denial.

"At first, there was no reaction. You were much like the new widow whose feelings during the first period after her husband's death are absent of emotions. For her, the reality of his death hasn't set in yet. She still feels married and maintains an identity with her husband.

"Reality hadn't set in for you either. Like the widow, you still retained your Mormon identity. You felt like a Mormon, and you still thought like one. Mentally you still had one foot in the Mormon Church even though the other foot was in Christianity."

"But," Judy interrupted, "if I was so oblivious to what was taking place, what brought on my insomnia?"

"Down deep," I said, "your unconscious knew what was happening. It knew you were about to lose everything you loved and all that gave meaning to your life."

"Are you saying," Judy asked, "that a year later my argumentative nature and defense of former beliefs is because I don't want to give up Mormonism? That I want to go back?"

"Not exactly. Your arguing and defensive stance is your psyche's way of fighting the loss. You're now in the stage called 'protest and anger.'

"A widow also protests her husband's death by continuing to talk about him as if he were still alive. She becomes mad if someone tries to point out he's dead. It's her way of hanging on to her husband. Defending former beliefs is your way."

I reached over and refilled both our glasses. "Judy," I said sympathetically, "when the husband is gone, the widow's essential needs are no longer being filled. Yours are no longer being filled either. The death of your cult cut off your supply. No longer does it maintain your identity, offer you security, explain your roots, set your goals, or establish your self-image. Everything the cult gave you has died. This has to evoke a serious crisis—not only consciously but unconsciously.

"Since," I continued, "this kind of loss threatens one's inner self, it leaves one feeling helpless and empty. When bereaved spouses want to overcome this emptiness, they seek another partner and remarry. You too, in a way, have sought another partner—Christianity. But, even as it takes time to adjust to a new marriage partner, it takes time to adjust to a new faith."

"But how *long* are these miserable feelings and behavior going to continue?" Judy asked, nearly on the verge of tears. "I don't know if I can continue without falling to pieces. I mean, it's really stressing me out!"

"Give yourself time, Judy. You haven't been in your new church long enough to replace what you've lost. Until Christian identity, security, and beliefs take root in your life, you'll continue to be in this state of anxiety.

"But understand," I continued, "you're not in this state because unconsciously you want to go back to the Mormon Church. Neither is it because God is telling you to go back. It's because you've become empty of basic essentials. Psychologists say these essentials are the psychological equivalents of food and drink. Since the cult fed you for many years, you're famished. Now you must look to Christ. You must not only drink in what the church has to offer, but learn to feed yourself by reading the Word daily. You have to get used to a new kind of food."

The sudden brilliance of the patio lights startled us. "Well," I said, glancing at my watch, "my automatic timer is right on schedule." We rose from our chairs and started back through the kitchen.

"I've practically taken up your whole afternoon," Judy said apologetically.

"It's all right," I said, smiling. "I needed a break."

As we weaved around the boxes and headed out the front door, Judy asked, "Does it take everyone the same length of time to go through these stages?"

In order to answer her question, I told her about Crinkle's death. I explained how the loss took Linda, Kimberly, and myself through the predicted stages—but all at different paces.

"For example," I said, as we walked toward her car, "two months after the funeral, seven-year-old Kimberly, despite the fact she participated in Crinkle's burial, insisted Linda include dog food on the grocery list. She was still in stage one—shock and denial. Linda, on the other hand, recovered from stages two and three, the anger and crying bouts, and spent time talking with me—reliving the good times she and Crinkle had growing up together. She was in stage four—voidness and resolving the loss. For myself, I had advanced to stage five—acceptance and adjustment—I was already thinking about a new dog for them.

"No one knows, Judy, how long you'll stay in your present stage. It varies with each person. It depends upon your personality, how long you were in the cult, and how active and devoted you were. It will also depend upon the help you receive and your ability to accept your loss and grieve. Give yourself time. You're participating in a healing process that can't be accelerated."

"What's my next stage?" Judy asked.

"Despair and final grief," I replied. "But brace yourself. It will probably be more difficult than the one you're presently in. You'll experience deep despair and sadness and do a lot of crying."

"That's comforting," Judy said forlornly.

"Well, there's one ray of hope," I said. "It's the final grieving process before the last emotional letting go. From there on it gets easier."

Judy was quiet for a minute. Then, with startling change of presence, her face lit up. "I know exactly how I'll get through stage three! Maybe even skip it! All I need to do is figure out what's taking place, step by logical step. If you'll write the details of stage three on a piece of paper, I'll analyze them. Then I'll go through each symptom in my mind, theoretically ascertain what's accomplished by each, then avoid the emotions . . ."

"Whoa, Judy!" I exclaimed, "that won't work! That's a common ploy of psychotherapy patients. They intellectualize the experience in order to avoid their feelings. The only thing you'll end up doing is repressing your emotions. Your grief has got to be experienced and resolved, or you'll become locked in."

Standing by the curb, I explained that stage three has four kinds of unresolved grief: (1) delayed grief, where the loss is denied for months or years with grief coming later; (2) inhibited grief, where mourning is repressed, resulting in physical and psychological symptoms; (3) prolonged mourning, where one clings to and takes comfort in the grief; and (4) intellectualizing, where one replaces feelings by an abstract, intellectual analysis of the problem.

"Does the last one sound familiar, Judy?"

"Yes," she said as she got into her car. She shut the door and turned the motor on. "Thanks so much for everything," she said, with tears in her voice. "I hope I get through this and come out in one piece. What if I don't?"

"You will, Judy. Because," I laughed, "you're looking at someone who went through it and lived to tell the tale!" Judy, half smiling, studied me for a second, then drove away.

Although Judy spent one-and-a-half years in stage two, the duration was short compared to others. She had an even rougher time when stage three hit—but, so did Elizabeth.

I accidentally ran into Elizabeth at a singles retreat. Because of vacation schedules and Labor Day, our home meetings had been postponed. I hadn't seen her for two months.

The camp, fifty miles from town, was nestled among green pines and waterfalls. It was just what I needed. From appearances, it looked like Elizabeth needed it too.

It was after dinner when I saw her walking towards the creek. She didn't see me until I called. She looked pleased, but there was something depressing in her demeanor.

"I didn't expect to see you up here," I said when I caught up with her. "But you look awfully worn out." She only shrugged her shoulders.

We headed toward the creek and sat down by the water's edge. I began making light conversation, speaking of the conference and that we would be resuming our own meetings in a couple of weeks. Then quietly she spoke. Her face was haggard and drawn, her voice constricted.

"He's gone from my life," she said slowly. "It's finally and really over."

"Who?" I said, suspecting who she meant.

"Father—that is, Reverend Moon," she corrected herself.

"But," I said, "you knew that when you left the cult, didn't you?"

"Maybe I did—maybe I didn't."

"I thought you were convinced their doctrine was wrong— that Reverend Moon couldn't possibly be the Messiah."

"I was! I was!" she burst out crying. "And I believe Christianity is right. But I miss everything I had. For a while I pictured Reverend Moon sending friends to find me. They'd say, 'Father's made changes—you'll like things the way they are now. We want you back. You're family.'

"But," she said apologetically, "at the same time I'm saying this, I don't mean I really want to go back. I'm just confused and sad—and don't understand why." She looked away, her eyes full.

"You don't have any more 'what-if' questions, do you?" I inquired. "Like, 'What if Reverend Moon is *really* the Messiah?'"

"No," she wiped her eyes with the bottom or her shirttail, "I don't believe he is anymore."

"Then why," I asked, "should you miss someone you don't believe in anymore?" I knew this was an unfair question. But, I wanted to see if she remembered what we covered in one of our group's get-togethers.

She slowly shook her head in the negative. I jogged her memory by reiterating the meeting where the stages of loss and grief were discussed. I reminded her of Myra who, at that time, was having a difficult time with stage three.

"Do you remember," I said, "how Myra admitted she was no longer plagued with what-if questions such as, What if Joseph Smith really did see the Father and Son . . . What if the *Book of Mormon* really was delivered by an angel? Do you remember her new symptom? How she was overcome with a deep, unbearable sadness that she had difficulty explaining or describing?"

"Yes, but I didn't get the impression it was as bad as what *I'm* going through!"

"Elizabeth, each one thinks their own problems are worse. But you're in the same stage as she was, and you're having the very same feelings. Like Myra, you're realizing your old life is slipping away for good. It's like a part of you is dying. And, in a way, it is—and you don't want to let go. You force yourself into remembering how good it used to be, in spite of what made you leave. You reminisce about Reverend Moon being the second Messiah—and wish he were. You relive the strong sense of cause and mission, the bonding with members, the excitement of positions held. But even so, I don't think you could go back. Do you?"

Elizabeth leaned forward, picked up a twig, and tossed it into the water. She was quiet for a long time as she watched it twist and turn until it disappeared downstream.

"No," she finally said. "I couldn't go back, even if I had the opportunity. It's not a part of my life anymore. I've got too much Christian teaching in me."

"There's another reason for your grief, Elizabeth, something else you're suffering from which may be of some consolation to you.

"When you were in the cult, you so sincerely believed it was the truth, that it triggered a deeper level of spirituality than you ever experienced before. It touched the inner core of your soul with an exciting devotion which was new to you.

"But now your drive has dwindled. The strong dedication that motivated you and upon which you thrived is gone. The dynamics that were a by-product of everything you believed are also gone. It's natural to miss all that. And you haven't replaced it yet."

Elizabeth heaved a big sigh. "Even though you've given me an explanation, I can't stop the sadness," she said. "I'm depressed—can't sleep at night—I avoid others—and I cry a lot. Someone talked me into coming to this retreat, but it hasn't helped. All I can think about is what I've lost. I feel like something has died in me and I'll never be the same again. It's all gone. Everything is *really* over . . ."

I reached over and took her hand. "Take my word for it, Elizabeth, this sadness will pass. In time, you're going to be a happy, excited Christian. Once you get into the Bible more and enter into church activities, the dynamics of genuine dedication, love, and zeal will be renewed in Christ.

"I can't make this stage any easier or shorter for you," I added. "It's something you're going to have to work through yourself. But God will help—and I'm here if you need me."

Elizabeth smiled and wiped her eyes. We prayed by the water's edge, and the presence of the Holy Spirit bore strong witness that God would indeed see her through. (She spent two years in stage three before moving on.)

It was also rough for Myra. The acute sense of emptiness which came in stage four, *voidness and resolving the loss,* made her extremely insecure. She became very dependent upon me and used any excuse to come to my home. When group meetings concluded she always hung back, spending as much as another hour. There were times when I caught myself resenting the intrusion upon my time, and it required all my patience. But, knowing that the best way a widow resolves her loss is talking about her dead husband, I assumed Myra needed to talk about her dead cult. So I encouraged it.

At first she spent a great deal of time talking about the excellence of Mormon Church programs, its high ideals and standards—every good thing she could think of. She was much like the widow forming a later image of her "perfect" husband— devoid of anything unfavorable. Because of this idealization of the Mormon Church, her remarks often included criticism of her new church because it didn't measure up.

Gradually, however, Myra began to recall the negative features of Mormonism which made her leave—her growing sense of control by leaders; the requirement of blind faith and unquestioned obedience; hypocrisy of Ward leaders in moral standards and business practices; similarities between pagan rituals and the Mormon temple ceremony (mostly gleaned from Judy); and Bible interpretations which she now recognized were out of context. Whether she was in the positive or negative mode, both caused her pain.

What she needed was to work through her feelings, resolve the fallacies of Mormonism, and hear me corroborate the truth of Christianity. I allowed her to express whatever she felt. Later, as she passed into stage five, *acceptance and adjustment,* she was able to remember comfortably, with no pain (although nostalgia), both the pleasures and disappointments of the lost relationship.

Melanie, on the other hand, spent three years in stage three because of repressed feelings. This probably contributed to the sores on her legs. She locked herself into the *inhibited grief* phase of this stage, due to three factors: (1) her own nature which tended to cover up feelings; (2) guilt about mourning a religion considered evil by Christian peers; and (3) wanting to put on a good front for the sake of acceptance.

Richard, however, was difficult to assess. He did not share all his private feelings. Although he contributed to our discussions, he persisted in being stoic. Since I didn't know Richard when he first came out of the Hare Krishnas, it was never clear how long he spent in stages one and two. He did, however, lock himself into stage three's *delayed grief* phase. Three years later, he entered stage four.

Judy, despite my warning, fell victim to the *intellectualizing* phase of stage three by replacing her feelings with an abstract, intellectual analysis of her problems.

However, with insomnia and nervousness increasing, she finally found it too difficult to maintain her detached attitude. It was then she gave in and acknowledged her grief. An agonizing six months followed, making a total of only sixteen months in this stage.

She felt that because of the severity of her mourning she came out of stage three faster than most. She claimed God put her through a "crash course" so she could become useful in her church sooner. She also claims to have skipped stage four.

Fortunately, none of the group went into *prolonged mourning*. In this phase, resolution may never occur. The former cultist clings to his grief, finds comfort in it, and continues to idealize his or her former religion.

Each felt, however, that because of the length of time spent in stages two and three, they must be having an emotional breakdown. Severe depression was common and they often felt like giving up. Emotions were so problematic they had thoughts of returning to the cult. Two made definite statements they would. The miracle was that none of them did.

How Can Christians Help?

1. *Understand the ex-cultist's emotions.* The cult filled many basic needs that provided a strong sense of security. Losing security of any kind always provokes an emotional reaction. This is because security is an instinctive need automatically instilled in a human being during one's nine-month experience in the womb.

According to some psychologists, ejection from the womb and being thrust out from the protective security supplied by "mother" is an unconscious devastation everyone carries with them. Recapturing that state of primal union or the fostering environment of the womb is the unrecoverable state for which all yearn to return.

In view of these innate needs, it is no wonder individuals are attracted to cults. They find in the cult a replication of the womb. Cults try to duplicate the love and security experienced by a young child still in the arms of its mother. Members are nurtured, made to feel safe, and are free from making decisions. A cultist often says he feels "warm and protected." And with the leader acting as mother/father substitute and the source of love and comfort, a cultist's affectionate response has to be expected.

However, when the leader rejects the cultist and friends who earlier claimed to be his "family" also turn their backs on him, it is a loss that is felt to the very core. The death of one's own mother could not be more devastating. To be thrust away from the cult is like being expelled from the womb all over again.

The anxiety is so severe that Dr. Saul V. Levine, in *Radical Departures*, says: "More than fifty percent of former members of radical groups show signs of emotional upheaval severe enough to warrant treatment during the first few months after their return."[5]

2. *Consider the ex-cultist's stages of loss and grief as comparable to a spouse losing a mate.* A widow, in addition to mourning for her husband, also mourns for herself. She mourns the identity she gained through being his wife—"I am Mrs. Don Smith." In like manner, the ex-cultist also mourns the loss of identity—"I am a Mormon." Neither one can say that anymore. In addition, some spouses have said, "You never get over the death; you just learn to live with it." For many former cultists, this is also true.

3. *Consider the stages of loss as comparable to one who is terminally ill.* When an individual is told he is dying, he realizes it not only means his personal existence will cease, but his continued usefulness—he will no longer be needed. Similarly an ex-cultist views himself as terminal. There are aspects of his inner self which he believes will die now that he's a Christian—especially the utilization of his talents.

Judy, always active in teaching adult classes, believed this. After leaving the Mormon Church, she told of recurring dreams full of sadness, despair, and uncontrollable crying because she felt no one in a traditional church would ever let an ex-cultist teach. Teaching had been her whole life—her ultimate identity had been gained from it. Life now had no meaning—her teaching days were over—her talents might as well be dead. She therefore mourned her own passing. Part of her attitude stemmed from the fact that the first church she entered did not believe in women teaching adult classes (this is not true of all churches).

4. *Understand the difference between anxiety over the death of an entity that definitely ceases to exist and the death of something that continues on.* In contrast to the death of a loved one where the deceased has physically left this sphere, there is the kind of death where the deceased one still remains. For example, when a child loses a parent through separation or divorce—to the child it is like a death. But, because the parent remains alive, adjustment becomes difficult if not impossible.

Similarly, the new believer's separation from her cult is like a death. But like the child, the former cultist is fully aware that the cult remains alive. This keeps her from finalizing its death. Both the child and the ex-cultist exhibit the same symptoms—anxiety, helplessness, and anger.

5. *Understand psychosomatic ailments.* Resisting a loss experience can be physically disastrous. As molecules in frozen water expand and have the power to burst steel pipes, says Ann Kaiser Sterns in *Living Through Personal Crisis,* even so do frozen emotions assume a power which can burst the body and cause physical problems.[6]

Psychosomatic problems for a bereaved spouse are shock, crying, sighing, throat tightness, laryngitis, digestive disturbances, headaches, backaches, insomnia, moodiness, irritability, fatigue, poor memory, allergic reactions, anxiety attacks, heart palpitations, dizziness, shortness of breath, anger, despair, weakness, and skin eruptions. The ex-cultist may exhibit some of these.

6. *Do not expect the ex-cultist to reject his "history."* Losses will always be remembered. A former cultist cannot cut his history out of his life. To do so is mentally, emotionally, and physically

impossible. The brain cells have recorded it—it's there to stay. Successful passage through the mourning stages must be accompanied with a healthy acceptance of who and what one is and was.

7. *Assure the ex-cultist it is acceptable to grieve.* It is important for former cultists to experience their emotions. Christians, rather than teaching that anger, bitterness, and depression are unacceptable, can help most by accepting human feelings as such.

8. *Understand the length of time.* Don't expect a fast recovery. Time spent in all stages, both for the widow and the ex-cultist, may vary from three to eight years. The lengthy process of resolution for the new convert is not because the "devil" still has hold on him, as some teach. Rather, it is the difficulty of breaking the psychological ties and adjusting to the void after many years of need-fulfillment.

9. *Be honest with the new convert about the church community.* "The longing desire for the warm and understanding total community is the search for the good mother," says Avery Dulles, "which is bound to end in disappointment and heartbreak."[7] Explain that one's new church is *not* going to be the perfect human community. Although the cult possibly failed in this respect, the former cultist may still expect fulfillment of this fantasy.

10. *Be patient and sympathetic.* Listen and talk about the cult in an understanding, nonjudgmental way. Do not minimize the ex-cultist's grief nor the length of time he or she spends in the stages. They constitute a necessary, though painful process leading to restitution. The former cultist does need to be watched, however, so he or she doesn't become locked into the stage of prolonged mourning.

11. *What new believers need to keep them from returning to the cult.* First, ex-cultists need to be shown unconditional love. The lament of those longing to return to the cult is, "They loved me just the way I was." It is the singular attraction which entices one to join a cult. On the other hand, those staying in the church often admit that it is only the joy and professions of

love shown by Christians that keep them from leaving and going back.

Second, if the new convert is to continue in the church with hope for the future, he needs to be informed about the stages of loss and grief. Knowing about them ahead of time helps. Third, the former cult member needs Christians who will provide the necessary outlet by inviting him to share openly without fear of criticism. If he does not feel free to share, his "grief [can become] solitary torment," says one author.[8]

Fourth, he needs to be convinced that the Bible is the Word of God. Faith comes by hearing; therefore, it is imperative that the former cultist hear it—not just from the pulpit, but on a one-to-one basis. Constant friendship with someone who continually shares God's love both by example and proclaiming the Word has a profound effect. It will give the new believer a lifeline to cling to throughout his bereavement.

Richard, Elizabeth, Judy, Melanie, and Myra's postcultic depression eventually dissipated. When they reached stage five, *acceptance and adjustment,* they were ready to move on. As they participated in church activities, acquired a new sense of self, and were asked to serve in positions (a crucial need discussed in chapter 10), they were able to give one hundred percent commitment to their new church and friends.

Overcoming the stages of loss and grief is a major hurdle for the former cultist. But when done, it doesn't mean all dilemmas are solved. There are still perplexing problems ahead. One is the sudden and unexpected devastation of finding roots, identity, and story destroyed. Divested of myths, clanship, and traditions, the new convert is left destitute as his world collapses.

Chapter 4 Notes

1. Susan Rothbaum, "Between Two Worlds: Issues of Separation and Identity After Leaving a Religious Community," in *Falling From the Faith,* ed. David G. Bromley (Newbury Park, CA: Sage Publications, 1988), 205.

2. Ann Kaiser Stearns, *Living Through Personal Crisis* (Chicago: The Thomas More Press, 1984), 49.

3. Clara Shaw Schuster and Shirley Smith Ashburn, *The Process of Human Development* (Boston: Little, Brown and Company, 1980), 789.

4. Ibid., 789–790.
5. Saul V. Levine, *Radical Departures: Desperate Detours to Growing Up* (San Diego: Harcourt Brace Jovanovich, 1984), 151.
6. Stearns, 81.
7. Avery Dulles, *Models of the Church* (Garden City: Doubleday, 1974), 57.
8. "Death & Remembrance," in *Birth, Adolescence, Marriage Death: The Journey of Our Lives, Life* special issue: (October 1991): 73.

5

LOSS OF ROOTS, STORY, AND IDENTITY

Explaining the ex-cultist's disorientation

I feel like I've been dematerialized," moaned Melanie, as she looked up at me from the chair on my front porch.

This was the strange statement I was greeted with as I arrived home and found her waiting for me.

"What on earth do you mean?" I asked, as my glance took in her forlorn expression.

"You know, formless, invisible, unconnected, like—well, do you ever watch Star Trek?"

Unlocking the front door, she followed me into the house while I unloaded my armful of packages. Motioning toward the patio, we went outside. With a significant sigh, Melanie slumped into one of the lawn chairs.

"Well, what's this all about," I prodded. "And what on earth does it have to do with Star Trek? Are you saying," I laughed, "that you're advancing so fast in the church that you feel you're in warp drive?"

Her exasperated look quickly sobered me.

"I know I've come a long way already," she began, "but something still isn't right, and I can't put my finger on it. The only way I can describe it is to use the transporter room on the starship *Enterprise* as an example—even if it is a TV show."

"Okay—I'm with you so far," I said.

"Well," she began, "to transport from the planet's surface to the ship, coordinates are set and one's body is dematerialized, beamed up, then rematerialized. But sometimes something goes wrong. If something is amiss with the coordinates, the particles of the person's body never stabilize. They try to materialize but can't. They fade in and out, indicating the person is lost in a disassembled state somewhere."

"Go on," I said.

"Well, that's the way I feel in the church. I keep asking myself, Who am I? What am I? Where do I belong?" There was a pitiable quiver in her voice.

"I don't have answers to these questions," she continued, nearly on the verge of tears, "because I don't feel I have any identity. I'm still floating around 'out there,' shapeless—in a state of nonmaterialization. It's an awful feeling!" she said. "I don't know what the problem is."

Heaving another deep sigh, she said, "I'm sure I must be a disappointment to God. Why can't I be like other Christians, all serene . . . untroubled . . . smiling all the time?"

Reaching for her hand I gently patted it. "They didn't come out of a cult," I said quietly. With that, she burst into tears.

As I tried to comfort her, I marveled at her ability to find the appropriate analogy. Fortunately, I was a "Star Trek" fan and could visualize the 7UP-like-bubbles of Star-Trekkian body particles trying to materialize. What was more fortunate was that I understood what Melanie was really trying to say. Her concerns struck a responsive chord in my own heart.

Her problem? She had lost the three most critical ingredients to maintaining a stable life: roots, story, and identity.

Mormonism offered a strong sense of these fundamental components. But when Melanie left the Mormon Church, she gave them up. Christians had told her—and rightly so—that her former roots and identity were no longer valid. But to suddenly lose such powerful stabilizers without having had time yet to firmly establish new ones left her suddenly empty. When this happens, there is only one way to describe how an ex-cultist feels—alone.

To suffer this kind of "aloneness" leaves a new convert totally destitute. A sense of derangement prevails that Melanie aptly described as formlessness and nonmaterialization. It causes such serious repercussions, not to mention barrenness of soul, that although former cultists are unable to analyze why they are so miserable, they seem to sense that returning to the cult will alleviate the problem. When one imagines herself or himself returning, the joyous feelings are often described as "coming home." I knew this from my own experience. I had to keep Melanie from considering this option.

Wiping her eyes with the Kleenex I offered her, Melanie began rubbing her temples.

"I don't think there's any hope for me. Why isn't this any easier?" she moaned. "Or," she said abruptly looking up, "do you even know what I'm trying to say?"

"Melanie, I think that what you are saying, in 'Trekkian' terminology of course," I smiled, "is that you gave up the cult's 'coordinates' to 'beam' into Christianity. Disengaged from them during transit, but not being firmly grounded in the church yet, you have no strong coordinates to lock you in. As a result, you fade in and out between the two worlds with materialization not taking place."

"That's exactly what I'm saying!" Melanie said with delight. "But," she added, "I'm not really sure what the *coordinates* are, yet it seems they're critical to my materialization."

"Coordinates," I said, "are any set of numbers used to specify a particular location—like the two coordinates of latitude and longitude. Therefore, the location coordinates to 'beam' someone into a starship pulls together the disassembled particles of the person's body, stabilizes them, and materializes them at the new location."

"But," Melanie interrupted, "what are they in my case?"

"Simple." I replied. "God designed in all human beings a set of three stabilizers so people can function as well-adjusted individuals. They are *roots, story,* and *identity*—the most powerful coordinates a person can lock into. And you've lost yours."

I proceeded to explain to her that *roots,* spiritual or physical, tell an individual or a group where they came from, why they're here, how they started, why they do the things they do, and why they are who they are. In any culture this is achieved through myths and stories from one's ancestors, heritage, national heroes or, as in Melanie's case, the Mormon culture.

Through its myths and sacred stories, Melanie acquired a powerful sense of roots—roots that dug deep, not only into the modern day Mormon church's story, but back beyond the individual stories of Joseph Smith, Christ, Moses, Adam, to eternity past. According to Mormon teaching, she was biologically conceived by God and a heavenly mother in a pre-mortal world. She had brothers and sisters with Jesus as her elder brother. She indeed had a unique identity—she had divinity flowing through her veins! She was taught in that world that she had a mission to come to earth. And someday she would return "home." Through this and other myths, she acquired roots and a well-established identity.

Stories are of three kinds. First, there are the myths and history of a culture's heritage and heroes which confirm and perpetuate the roots. These determine how people and cultures live, how they behave, and how they treat themselves, the world, others, and God.

Secondly, there is the story of the individual community itself—how members relate to that culture with their common problems and how they overcome them.

Thirdly, there is one's own individual story within the culture. This generally consists of accumulated childhood experiences containing the negative and positive, the triumphs and tragedies. It also includes a vast array of input from people, places, and situations. In Melanie's case, she acquired her story as a result of input from cult leaders, friends, myths, doctrines, standards, and also through her selfless dedication, service, faith experiences, and love for her religious culture.

Identity, on the other hand, is the assurance individuals, cultures, or nations gain as a result of having both roots and story. Identity confirms one's existence, gives assurance that one's everyday world coheres in meaning, and shows that humanity has a purposeful destiny. It promotes self-esteem and a positive self-image, collectively as well as individually. Without it, individuals are strangers to themselves and to others.

As a result of strong Mormon roots, story, identity, and a tightly framed network of relationships, Melanie had confidence, security, wholeness, well-being, and a good self-image. She felt useful and needed. She knew exactly where she came from, what she was, who she was, why she was here on earth, what her mission was, and where she was going.

After explaining this to Melanie, I said, "All three stabilizers of *roots, identity,* and *story* tell individuals that they did come from somewhere and that their life is meaningful. This is what you developed through the Mormon culture."

"Wow!" Melanie gasped. "That's a lot of stuff I never thought of before. I wonder which loss—roots, story, or identity—I'm suffering from the most?"

"No way to determine that," I responded. "They are so closely intermeshed and so dependent upon each other that it's impossible to distinguish them once they've been fused into an individual. It's like mixing paints. The artist can have blue and yellow paint lying separately on a palette, but after mixing them together to make green, there is no way the artist or anyone else can look at the green and distinguish the blue and yellow anymore. The colors which combined to make the green are so interdependent upon each other that they are inseparably linked.

"Similarly, your cult stabilizers, like the mixing of paints, blended together and contributed to a singular result. But your green world has now been destroyed, and you have entered a world of another color—say purple. However, you're not fully 'purple' yet, because it takes a blending of certain colors, meaning certain coordinates, that haven't fully fused in you yet. They're lying on your palette waiting to be combined. Yes, you know you have Christ, and you intellectually know about Christian roots, story, and identity, but you're not fully grounded in all of them yet.

"All you can do at best, Melanie, is hope to see the importance of these coordinates and recognize that the loss of them fits into the total picture of your disorientation.

"So, to wrap it all up, your combined Mormon roots, story, and identity were your *coordinates*. Now they're gone. Without them, and with no new ones firmly established yet, you can't materalize and function. Does that sound right?"

Melanie suddenly sagged back into her chair and sighed with relief, "That's it!"

During the the week, Melanie was elated after having her unique experience clarified. She repeated it to Judy, who related it to Richard, who then told Elizabeth and Myra. Excited that someone had so definitively described their common experience, they were anxious to see the next episode of Star Trek. They watched for an incomplete beaming-aboard so they could say, "Yep—that's how it is!"

Our next meeting proved fruitful. Not only was the group intrigued with the Star Trek analogy, but they were beginning to more fully understand about roots, identity, and story. Strangely enough, it came about as a result of popcorn. Richard surprised everyone by bringing two large bags. Digging my popper out of a downstairs closet, we poured in the kernels and stood around watching it do its thing.

We made five batches, dumping them into a large kettle. After allaying everyone's concern whether I was putting on enough butter, we piled our bowls full and went into the front room.

The enjoyment of watching the popcorn triggered all kinds of memories. Richard and the others began relating stories which in some way were connected with popping corn. There were family gatherings, stories told by parents and grand-parents, stories told at the dinner table, and stories that explained family tragedies.

Myra recalled her Mormon "Family Nights." "We had flannel board stories, puppet shows and songs," she said, "and we each contributed something in the way of talent. Sometimes it was pretty amateurish, but we all laughed and had a good time. And, if we didn't pop corn at the end, we figured the whole thing was a flop!"

Quickly seizing the opportunity, I said, "All these popcorn stories, without your realizing it, have permanently affected you. They're part of your history, your story. And it's out of them that you live and interpret the world."

"Is this part of the roots-identity-and-story thing?" Elizabeth asked.

"Exactly," I replied.

"Well," Elizabeth began, "I can understand how childhood stories influence me as an adult, but how does one live out of a story in a religion?"

"There are three kinds of stories in religion," I began. First, ancient stories which predate the establishment of a religious culture; secondly, the story which that culture eventually spins out about itself and, thirdly, one's own personal story as a participant.

"First, I'll tell you about the kind that began thousands of years ago and helped to form communities where people gathered together, broke bread, and told their culture's stories. Some ancient cultures told myths of how the world is supported on the back of a giant turtle or how the sun is drawn across the daytime sky in a chariot, subject to a monster who swallows it at night.

Israel did the same thing but told factual stories carefully based upon God's dealing with their ancestors. Later, when Israel formed a nation, these stories became sacred, like Noah and the Ark. While the stories of most religious cultures claim to be sacred, what made Israel's sacred stories valid was they contained revealed truths that God wanted Israel to know and live by. To further establish their legitimacy, they were preserved in writing by authors who received inspiration from God, thus giving them divine trustworthiness.

"Stories were the only method that could answer certain questions like, What's happening to us? Why did our forefathers do what they did? How and why has God dealt with us the way He has? What does God expect of us?

"When the Israelites questioned whether God was going to save them, the prophets always went back to the basic stories of Genesis and Exodus. Through these they reaffirmed their roots and identity, remembered God, and strengthened themselves by listening. It created a bond which drew them together, thus creating the second kind of story—their own community's story.

"Stories always integrate individual lives into a greater reality. They help individuals to achieve meaning and purpose, interpret life, dictate how to respond to problems, and sustain the individual in the face of challenges.

"The Israelites, by living out their stories, also created a second kind of story—their own unique story as a culture. And, of course, each individual member had his or her own story of what it personally meant."

"Give us a specific example in New Testament times," Elizabeth asked.

"The New Testament Gospel itself is a story, the good news of God's redeeming work through Jesus Christ. It is the story of not only Jesus' life, death, and resurrection, but also the effect of that 'good news' upon a community of believers. God inspired the New Testament writers to accurately record this story and thereby demonstrate through the history of the New Testament church how the Holy Spirit pulled together the patterns of their lives after the crucifixion and resurrection. The Church was formed out of the Gospel story, and it lived out that story in daily experience.

"Another example is Mark. Mark contains stories of what Jesus did which proved who He was, and believers live out His stories. Matthew and Luke relay parables to us—stories with double meanings, intended to make truth more engaging and thought-provoking.

"Stories always do it best. Even Jesus, rather than telling people abstract, metaphysical aspects about the Godhead, told stories—a certain man went down from Jerusalem to Jericho—the Kingdom of Heaven is like a treasure hid in a field—and people lived out His stories. Thus, the second story creates the third kind of story, the individual's story.

"Now, cults do the same thing. They also tells stories about their founders, ancient prophets, hidden revelations, and divine callings to those revelations. While it claims its stories are inspired, they can't be for God was already speaking to Israel and the New Testament church. Since He has already spoken through the Scriptures, He cannot be speaking through the various cult 'Bibles.' God is not the author of confusion.

"Nevertheless, cults promulgate stories which tell members who they are and what their mission is. And like the community of Israel, a cult not only tells a variety of stories but in the process creates its own story as a singular culture.

"So," I concluded, "cult believers, like any religious culture, including Christianity, also live out three kinds of stories: ancient stories which precede the cult; the cult's own story as a community; and the third kind, personal stories which develop from simply being a member. Through all three a person gains a particular perspective of God, others, and the world. "Now that you've entered Christianity," I concluded, "you have new stories to learn about and live."

"That's fascinating!" Judy said. "If stories affect us that deeply, that's got to explain why I had so many problems when I first entered Christianity. I was still looking through cult-colored glasses. As a result, I was interpreting, as well as expecting, the church community to be like a Mormon community. Yet, if I could give up doctrines, why couldn't I give up the stories?"

"Don't feel badly," I said. "People always seem to find more fulfillment in stories than they do doctrines."

Richard dejectedly shook his head. "How can a person be expected to undo everything that took years to develop—to live out of a new story in such a short time? If established Christians understood this better, maybe they wouldn't expect so much from us so soon."

"Or," Elizabeth sighed, "become disappointed in us so quickly."

"Elizabeth," I said, "I think the disappointment you sense is frustration within yourself. I don't believe Christians are disappointed in you. They're concerned and want the best for you no matter how long it takes. Anyone for more popcorn?"

Richard eagerly filled his bowl, then asked, "How can you tell," he asked, "if someone has developed roots?"

"You can always tell," I replied, "by listening to what they say. For example, 'My people came to America from Scotland . . . I'm of Israel because I was born of a Jewish woman . . . My grandfather was the first trapper in this state . . . My mother was born in New Jersey during the depression.'"

"Well, those statements," Richard interrupted, "are easy to understand, but how can you tell if a person in a *religion* has developed roots?"

I then explained that the "rooting" process in a religion first begins by its claim of having been started by someone of great spiritual stature like Buddha, Ascended Masters, or whomever.

Then members, believing this, become rooted and soon say, 'I belong to the true Israel,' or 'The man who started our group had a vision from God,' 'I had heavenly parents in a world before this one,' 'A ritual sealed me into the lineage of Christ,' 'I'm a literal descendant of Abraham because the Holy Ghost changed my blood type,' or 'I joined Judaism and now belong to the race God chose.'

"Although statements may vary," I said, "they all reflect the same thing—a secure sense of roots based on identifying with the original founder, his sacred calling, the organization's supposed initiation by God, and the sacred stories it perpetuates. One's identity is further acknowledged when the member proudly boasts, 'I'm a Mormon!', 'I'm a Hare Krishna!', or 'I'm a Moonie!'"

"If roots, story, and identity do all that," Myra interjected, "it's no wonder we become unglued when we lose them!"

"Some of us still are," moaned Elizabeth.

"Don't feel badly, Elizabeth," I said. "Giving up these kinds of fundamentals always creates a crisis. When it happens, one's world collapses with much the same effect as a child finding out there is no Santa Claus."

"Yep, that's what it's like," Elizabeth sighed, "only a hundred times worse."

"Let's drown our sorrows in more root beer," Richard grinned, trying to lighten the mood.

They piled into the kitchen again, and after all the popcorn they had consumed, it was hard to believe they were still hungry. Judy reached into the refrigerator and grabbed the macaroni salad she brought. Melanie poured a bag of tortilla chips into a bowl and opened some guacamole dip. I opened a can of black olives and watched them as they filled their plates and finished off the root beer.

"Did any of you see the *National Geographic* documentary on TV last week?" Richard queried, between mouthfuls. It was about an aboriginal race in Australia whose legends are so endangered they'll soon be lost to the new generation. After understanding this roots and identity thing, I believe I know what these tribespeople are going through."[1]

"I saw the same one," Judy chimed in as she swallowed down half a dill pickle and her last bite of salad.

"The show began," she said, perching herself on one of the kitchen stools, "by describing Gagudju laws, traditions, and rituals that were over 40,000 years old. It explained that they were on the verge of becoming extinct, not only because of twentieth-century inroads, but because they're known only to four elderly tribesmen. Once these tribesmen die, their whole culture will be lost to future generations. The Gagudjus will have no more ties to their own past.

"I couldn't quite understand," Richard interrupted, "why I felt such emotion. But now I believe it was genuine empathy over their loss of roots and story. And," he quickly added, looking over at me, "identity, affirmation, meaning, purpose, and significance. How's that?" he grinned.

"Very good, Richard," I laughed. "I also agree—it was a terrific show. However, there was something about the very last scene that I thought was particularly moving. To illustrate the race's desolation, it showed a lonely Gagudju boy of about twelve with spear in hand silhouetted against the evening sky, looking out over the plains of his ancestors. He was facing the new world of the twentieth century that would soon render his world devoid of myths and traditions, one in which ancestors would no longer speak to him. You couldn't help but sense the profound tragedy of a lost and dying culture, a people that would have no more 'story' to explain where they came from, who they belonged to, why they exist, or what their purpose is. It was very moving, to say the least."

"I now understand better," Judy said thoughtfully, "how each of our respective cults also had traditions, rituals, roots, stories, meaning, and purpose which we lived out of—all of which contributed to our identity. And for us, like the Gagudjus, it is all dying because we've entered a new world that requires us to give up these beliefs."

"But," I interjected, "lest we end on a low note, we need to remember what we gave up our former world for . . ." But before I could continue, Melanie spoke.

"I can understand losing membership in a tribe, but since we never belonged to a tribe, I wonder why we're suffering just as much as the Gagudjus?"

"Oh, Melanie, you did come from one!" I said.

She looked up, startled.

"The Mormon Church has a very strong sense of tribalism. In fact, they have a 'clan' mentality comparable to the Jews.

"Mormons," I continued, "call themselves 'modern Israel' and believe they descend directly from the 'loins and lineage' of Abraham, Isaac, and Jacob through Ephraim and Manasseh.[2] One of the major purposes of a Patriarchal Blessing is to tell you which *tribe* you came from."

"Gosh," Melanie said, "I forgot about that. You're right!"

"Of course, this isn't unique to the Mormon Church. Other Bible-oriented cults also trace some kind of lineage to ancient Israel. Herbert Armstrong's Worldwide Church of God uses the Anglo-Israelism theory which claims that Great Britain and the United States are the true Israel. Others also have their unique perspective on this theory, such as the 'I Am' Ascended Masters, the Aryan Nation, Church of Jesus Christ Christian, Neo-Nazism, and many other so-called identity groups.

"This tribalism," Judy said, "reminds me of a puzzling statement made by one author. He said that when one belongs to a tribe with its roots, common myths, and traditions, 'he does not so much live *in* a tribe; *the tribe lives in him.*'"[3]

"I relate to that," I said. "I believe this tribal-indwelling may account for the frustrated phrases new believers often use: 'I've got to get Mormonism out of me. When is *it* going to leave?'"

Judy mused, "Maybe that explains what happened to me a while back. Feeling I'd never get rid of Mormonism inside me, it nearly drove me crazy—especially at night. *It* kept telling me I had to remain true to my birthright. And *it* wasn't something I could leave and walk away from because it was *in* me. I had to wait for *it* to leave. I asked a Christian about this problem, but she interpreted 'it' as 'a devil,' so I didn't mention it again."

"Gosh," Myra said, "I wonder if that's what's been bugging me? Every now and then something inside of me makes me cry out to go back—and something inside of me *wants* to. But in my more rational moments I ask myself, *Why should I want this? I know Christianity is right.* But at night, when I drift in and out of sleep, it's *Mormonism, Mormonism,* tugging at me. Then I start thinking: *If only I could go back—but I can't. If only it were true—but it isn't.* I enjoyed the Mormon Church, I loved the church, I belong to it, I want to go back. But I can't—it's not biblical. Maybe the answer *is* 'tribalism.'"

As the evening continued, each person clarified his or her loss of roots, identity, and story as it related to their cult. Desperate to rid themselves of disoriented feelings and loss of identity, they concluded that the major *key*—and *only* key—was to constantly read the Bible. Although they knew it sounded simplistic, they believed that by reading the history of Israel as well as the New Testament period, a new sense of Christian "tribalism" would develop. In addition they would try to replace cult myths with Old and New Testament stories. They also felt that participation in their respective church communities would help to establish stronger roots and a new identity.

The evening proved to be a significant get-together, probably the best we'd had. I was grateful for our little group that was so intent on persevering and helping each other. I was truly blessed from listening to them. At the same time, however, I couldn't help but think of the hundreds of other ex-cultists who are not so fortunate—those who drifted in and out of churches: empty, formless, "dematerialized," as Melanie described, desperately needing to lock into stable coordinates.

How Can Christians Help?

1. *Understand how essential roots, identity, and story are and what it means to lose them.* By comprehending how deeply they are engrained and how intensely they contribute to a person's makeup, it will allow one to see that giving them up and trying to replace them will not be accomplished overnight.

2. *Direct the convert to new roots, story, and identity.* Until Christian roots are firmly planted, new identity established, and story developed (all of which take time), there are four avenues which will help during the interim:

a. Purpose and meaning are acquired through activity in the church. Ask the new convert (if ready) to participate not only in socials but in the church organization. Besides needing a substitute for the busy and active life led in the cult, the new believer needs to feel he or she is contributing to and is part of God's cause. (This may not be feasible at the convert's initial entry into the church.)

b. Establish identity through love and acceptance. Until the convert understands more fully his or her position in Christ (which is one's claim to authentic identity), love and caring from the community will carry him along.

    c. Establish identity through new friendships. Help the convert make new friends. Tell the new believer you understand the loss of former cult friends but emphasize that new friends will become just as meaningful.

    d. Establish identity and roots through a home fellowship Bible study. It is imperative that the new convert be in a situation where he relates to other Christians and hears them share a common faith in the Scriptures. The more he or she relates to group-sharing, the more roots and identity will begin to grow.

    3. *Lay the necessary groundwork to establish roots.* Convince the new believer that the Bible is really the divinely inspired Word of God. This is more important than trying to find proof texts which prove the cult false.

Clarify how the Old Testament foreshadows the New Testament church. Describe how Christ became the sacrifice once for all, that temple ordinances are done away with, and that Christ is the final revelation and no more is needed. It is not uncommon for former cultists to feel bitter disappointment that there is to be no more revelation than what is contained in the Bible. Being used to extra-biblical revelation and envisioning a greater "plan of salvation" for mankind as taught through their cult, their *private* lament will be—they may not voice this aloud—"Is this *all* there is to Christianity?"

Nevertheless, this groundwork will help set them on the path to being convinced of a necessary concept: the Old Testament and the New Testament were not foreshadowing the need for a new cult! To combat the cult's stand that God started the cult, you may find it necessary to learn Bible passages the cult uses to claim this.[4]

    4. *Lay the necessary groundwork to establish story.* Familiarize the new convert with Old and New Testament Bible stories, emphasizing their context in Israel's history. When applicable, bring out typologies which point to Christ. Help the ex-cultist see the thread running throughout the Bible of God's ultimate objective to reconcile man to Himself. Explain in simple

terms how a new convert is spiritually begotten and adopted into the family of God.

5. *Sympathize and show patience when the convert insists on clinging to former roots, story, and identity.* Explain to the ex-cultist that the reason he cannot let go is *not* because God is trying to tell him the cult is right but for other very human reasons: First, there is love for what was once near and dear to one's heart, which is always difficult to relinquish. Second, fear of stepping into the unknown always provokes a feeling of insecurity. This fear makes one revert to the past and cling to that which is more familiar. Assure the new believer you understand that he or she is going through a difficult time.

Melanie, Myra, Richard, Judy, and Elizabeth worked hard at analyzing their loss of roots, story, and identity. Effecting substitutes wasn't easy.

Myra, devastated over losing such fundamental components from her life, doubted that anything could ever replace them. Melanie was fearful her "Trekkie" feeling of "nonmaterialization" would be permanent. Elizabeth, discouraged most of the time, always needed prodding. Richard and Judy, however, looked at the assignments intellectually, believing systematic effort would pay off.

All in all, they were spurred on by realizing that: (1) they had passed the point of no return, so they had to press forward; (2) they belonged to a group of friends to which they were expected to relate their progress; and (3) recognizing their influence on each other, they didn't want to let each other down.

Four months later, they reported their progress. However, while listening to Judy and Elizabeth, I learned an important lesson—one which I had not learned until then.

Admitting how painful it was to lose former roots and identity, they felt they could reject their *cultural* story and the myths of their cult, but concluded there was no way they could reject their *own* story. More importantly, it wasn't necessary. Judy explained:

"I was intimidated by other Christians," she began. "I tried to slice the cult experience—my story—right out of my life as if it had never happened . . . as if the cult were so evil that it had no decisive factor in establishing the virtues and principles which are now part and parcel of my life. I tried to smother who I was.

"And who was I, really?" she continued. "I was a human being, albeit an ex-cultist, but who, by means of Mormon teachings, had acquired a good self-image, above average standards, and high ethics. I had a heart planted with images that to this day still produce dynamics which dictate how I treat myself, the world, others, and God.

"I'm a person who remembers, even with nostalgia, many of the good things about the cult and who has grown as a result of that experience. I am one who has her own way of worshiping and her own way of speaking. To pretend anything different would be a lie.

"I will still retain *my* story," she continued, "I have no intentions of rejecting it. Although I have a new identity as a Christian, part of that new identity will consist of what I used to be!" This struck a responsive chord with everyone.

Elizabeth, because of her shy nature, was hesitant but began speaking while her eyes brimmed over with tears. "Reverend Moon was my whole world. My adjustment period in a traditional church has been horrendous—the emotional repercussions beyond description. But I think I'm going to make it.

"No matter how many of my Christian friends would like to believe I have utter disregard and contempt for the cult, I will not nor cannot forget my time in it. For others to insist I eradicate the experience is wrong. Like Judy, I know it's impossible to totally obliterate one's own 'story' because both the good and bad are etched into every cell of my mind and body. The longer I try to erase that which was part of me, the longer it hinders me in becoming what I'm meant to be.

"I need to accept my story as happening—that it was an important part of my history and that it belongs there. My experience is what shaped me and, as a Christian at this moment in time, I *am* that story."

Everyone burst out in applause. Jumping to our feet, we threw our arms around her. We all knew Elizabeth didn't have a strong personality, and for her to formulate such a decisive conclusion and stand firmly for something was almost more than we could contain.

After their excitement subsided, Melanie shared. She said she felt that by forcing herself to participate in church activities and home Bible studies more, she was beginning to "materialize." She was finally locking into, she said with a grin, the right co-ordinates.

Richard's testimony, on the other hand, was not about his personal story. Rather, he described an experience that he claimed finally triggered Christian roots and story in him. First, he amazed everyone by how much of the Bible he had read. But more amazing was the experience he related.

"I don't know if I can put this in words," he began, "because it was actually a spiritual perception which came to me.

"I've been reading Old Testament stories, and previously the only way I saw them was as separate and distinct stories, although interesting and inspiring.

"Well, I was right in the middle of reading the other afternoon when all of a sudden, like the dramatic clashing of cymbals, the whole Israelite history suddenly unified! Every story—beginning with Adam and Eve, through Leviticus, Judges, Chronicles, Esther to Malachi—rather than containing isolated stories, harmonized! It was like I could see the hand of God orchestrating the whole thing toward a deliberate and final crescendo! And I saw what that crescendo was—and I was *part* of that crescendo! The whole history wasn't just for the Jews, but was also *my* history, *my* stories, *my* roots, *my* God, and *my* Jesus!"

We all sat for a moment in awe. And although he had claimed it was difficult to put into words, we all understood what had happened to him. Richard, always so factual, had received an outstanding experience, and it had changed him. And best of all, his unique experience held out a promise to the others. In due time, their emptiness would be replaced with Christian roots and identity, and it would become their story in a way that would become just as meaningful.

Judy's words closed our meeting: "Each one of us has our time and season," she said. "Richard has shown us that continual feeding on the Word will establish our foundation and help us acquire new roots, story, and identity. We need to press on and know that He who has begun this good work in us, will carry it on to completion." (Phil. 1:6)

During the next few months it appeared to them that they had passed the greatest hurdle of all. Although they had made great headway in giving up their former roots and identity and realized the process whereby they could establish new ones—and although they reconciled their personal story and looked forward to creating a new one—there was one story that each of their individual cults had purposely created that was difficult for them to resolve. Why? Because Christians seemed unable to give them a satisfactory answer.

This story, common to all cults, is so powerful that even after a former cultist has advanced through most of the stages of recovery, it comes back to taunt him later. This barrier to further growth is the subject of the next chapter.

Chapter 5 Notes

1. *National Geographic* TV special, aired February 13, 1988, Channel 7, San Antonio, Texas.
2. Every member's lineage is confirmed when one receives his or her Patriarchal Blessing by the laying on of hands and by a prophecy through which one's lineage is declared. Whites usually descend from Ephraim, American Indians from Manasseh, and Blacks from Cain and Ham. This Abrahamic lineage constitutes the elect, and the Mormon Church believes those today who find themselves drawn to convert to Mormonism will prove to be literal descendants of the elite line of Joseph.
3. Harvey Cox, *The Secular City* (New York: MacMillan Co., 1965), 10.
4. For the ex-Mormon, a thorough understanding of the following Scriptures is essential: Isaiah 29:1–4, 11–14; Revelation 14:6–7; Malachi 3:1; John 10:16; Genesis 49:22–26; and Ezekiel 37:15–20. To combat the cult's interpretation, an understanding of the context is imperative.

6

THE PRINCIPLES OF MASS MOVEMENTS

*How to combat the idea the
cult was started by God*

Myra stared at me with a kind of *I dare you* look. "The Mormon Church's continued success," she emphatically stated, "proves it was started by God, or else it would have died out!" Her declaration was a jolt that took me off guard.

It was Saturday afternoon, and I was rushing through the mall, anxious to keep another appointment. Hurrying through the food pavilion, I tried to ignore the aroma of freshly baked cinnamon rolls and the oriental delicacies, but my steps faltered in front of the pizzeria. I decided I had time.

As I was taking in the wedge-shaped slices with their rounds of pepperoni, chopped olives, and melted cheese, someone tapped me on the shoulder.

"Oh, hi, Myra," I smiled, turning around. "Looks like we have the same weakness, huh?"

Myra nodded with a feeble smile. "I tried to call you."

"Well," I said, ignoring my inclination to ask her what was wrong, "we might as well get something to eat and sit down." I rummaged through my purse for my wallet. "My treat, but I have to warn you, I'm in a hurry."

After paying for our pizzas, we headed for one of the small tables beneath the glass-domed rotunda. It was then she lowered the boom.

"Well?" Myra asked. "Do you have an answer for the Mormon Church's success? Can you explain why, if it's false, it hasn't died out?"

I sighed. I had almost forgotten how a former cultist could be gung ho for Christ one minute, then besieged with doubts the next.

"Oh, Myra," I instinctively said, "I thought you were doing so well!" It was the wrong thing to say. I should have known her question wasn't so much a challenge as a plea.

Myra bristled. "Well, the book of Daniel says the stone of God's kingdom would roll on and consume everything else until it filled the whole earth. Well, the stone sure didn't roll on during the Dark Ages when Christianity fizzled out! I haven't found a Christian yet who can reconcile that with the Mormon Church's membership of eight-and-a-half million!"[1]

I knew where she got her argument. Similar to other cults, the Mormon Church had purposely created a myth that its continued success proves a divine origin. So well grounded is this belief that it naggingly and persistently clings to the back of an ex-cultist's mind causing serious reservations about staying in Christianity.

Christians, trying to refute this claim, often say, "Your cult is successful because it's satanic, and Satan has great power." But, it isn't a convincing answer. I had to come up with something better. I needed to offer Myra an alternative view of her cult's longevity and success.

"I think we need something to drink," I quickly suggested. "7Up?" Myra nodded. As I weaved around potted palms and back toward the concession stands, I used the time to gather my thoughts. When I returned, she had mellowed somewhat.

"Of course," Myra began, "this doesn't mean I'm giving up on Christianity or losing my faith. I just, uh, need some answers, you know."

"Well, rest assured," I said, setting our drinks on the table, "there is an answer—one that will completely dismiss this erroneous idea. But, it's somewhat complex and takes more time than we've got here, especially in this noisy mall. However, let me say this.

"The claim of divine origin has nothing to do with a cult's success. There is one predominant reason for a cult's longevity. Now, admittedly there are other contributing factors, such as offering salvation by works rather than facing one's sinful condition, but I'm talking about a reason most are unfamiliar with.

"A cult's success, rather than being attributable to God's presence, is due to certain key principles which, if a cult follows, will automatically make it prosper."

"But what are they?" Myra questioned anxiously.

"Tell you what. I have an appointment, so I'll give them to you at our next meeting. If you're concerned about this, maybe the rest are too. In the meantime, go to the library and get Eric Hoffer's *True Believer* and read it. It's a small book. It'll prepare you for what I'm going to cover." I was relieved at her eagerness.

"I've got to go now," I said, looking at my watch. I gave her a pat on the back and flashed her a reassuring smile.

Dumping my food wrappers into a nearby refuse container, I headed for the exit. My mind was moving fast. I had lifted her depression, roused her interest, and now I had the chore of preparing material to answer one of the most crucial questions an ex-cultist can ask: *How can I explain my cult's apparent success if it isn't of divine origin?* The next day I poured over my books, including old notes taken from Hoffer's book. Finally I was ready.

As Myra came through the door that evening, she informed me she was halfway through Hoffer's book, and Melanie was on the waiting list. Richard, Judy, and Elizabeth also showed interest.

"I'm anxious to hear about this," Judy began. "Myra's question puzzles me too. I haven't met a Christian yet who can give a satisfactory answer. But," she grinned, "I rather suspect you've got one, judging from the pile of stuff you have on the table!"

"You're right," I said. "What I hope to give all of you is another way of viewing your cult's longevity and success.

"But first, I'd like to explain how I happened across Hoffer's book. I was browsing in a library shortly after I left the Mormon Church, and at that time I was struggling with this very same question. So, his book was a godsend.

"However, I have to warn you that while Hoffer has valuable insights on what generates a mass movement and why an organization continues to survive, I don't go along with his philosophical stance."

"Which is?" Judy asked.

"He doesn't state any. Rather, he has a very cold, Machiavellian detachment in his analysis of mass movements and the people who compose them. He portrays political expediency above morality and ascribes no divine inspiration to the success of Christianity. He views its success no differently than the success of any other organization. However, he appears to have purposely done this. In his own words, he admits his book 'passes no judgments, and expresses no preferences. It merely tries to explain.'[2] Perhaps he, as a new writer, thought his book would have more appeal by not expressing a personal opinion.

"But," I concluded, "he offers some good insights by describing the principles which are common to all movements. And when I compared the history of the Mormon Church to his analysis, I couldn't help but marvel at the way it applied. At least it offered a plausible answer for a cult's success.

"For Myra's sake, I'm going to use the Mormon Church as a model, but I'm sure Richard and Elizabeth will benefit from it too.

"Another reason for using the Mormon Church," I added, "is that no other American cult has grown as fast, and it's the best example of a cult extending beyond the first and second generation. In addition, I'm more familiar with Mormonism, and it would become too burdensome if I tried to cover the Hare Krishnas and the Unification Church, too. But since the principles apply to any cult movement, by the time we finish all of you will see that the claim of divine origin has absolutely *nothing* to do with a cult's prosperity."

We settled into the front room, and I began my presentation.

"Although there are many facets to what Hoffer presents, I'm only choosing certain highlights which I believe apply to this subject. His main thrust is that whether a movement is political, revolutionary, nationalistic, or religious, its success is inevitable as long as it applies certain principles in each of the predictable stages it will encounter. Since cults are movements, this applies to them as well.

"According to Hoffer, there are always special conditions that must precede each stage in order to make people receptive to a movement." Reaching for my chart which illustrated stages one and two, I placed it on the easel. "If these two stages come into existence," I said, "the rise of a movement is inevitable:

> Stage 1: *Lethargy, boredom, unrest, or a critical situation* from which people need to be delivered. They will have a strong desire for change.
>
> Stage 2: *A Need to find meaning, purpose, and hope through change.* If the need is because of lethargy, boredom, or unrest, then purpose and meaning will be achieved through finding a holy cause. If it is because of an existing crisis or dissatisfaction, they seek it through deliverance (which may be a new religion), or someone or thing which offers hope for change.[3]

Judy interrupted, "I think we're all more interested in religious movements. Can you give us an example of one in history that was started by these preconditions?"

Before I could speak, Richard jumped right in. "Sure, the Exodus!"

"Right on, Richard," I said, pleased. "And do you know the reason the Hebrews were willing to follow Moses? For them it wasn't boredom but dissatisfaction. Moses offered hope for change in the midst of their critical situation. And God allowed the critical situation to escalate for His own purpose. If they had been living peaceably in Egypt, had not been in bondage, and had not been in need of a deliverer, *nothing* could have made them leave for some promised land. Hope for change was the drawing card which made it possible for Moses to unite a bickering, disruptful, backbiting group into a successful movement.

"The same thing precipitated the early Christian movement. The Jews at the time of Jesus were also in crisis. They had been without a major prophet for four hundred years, and Roman rule was unbearable. This made the hope for a deliverer uppermost in their minds. They were ripe for a movement led by a long-awaited Messiah. If they had *not* been in crisis, there would have been no inclination to follow Jesus. They were, as Eric Hoffer states, hungry for a 'Man of Words' who would deliver them out of their situation. Once again, Hoffer to the contrary, God had His hand in that.

"Now, at the time of Joseph Smith, in 1823–1830, if anyone wondered about the future of his new group, one only needed to examine the prevailing conditions to know it would take hold. Just before Smith's movement started, a critical situation existed. This condition resulted from a mixture of many factors that demanded change—change that the people felt was crucial.

Judy interrupted. "But what *caused* this condition?"

"The inevitable aftermath," I said, "from the previous movement—America's two Great Awakenings from 1725–1825 which produced revival under such great men as Jonathan Edwards and George Whitefield.

"But as with all revivals, excitement eventually wanes and a period of boredom, dissatisfaction, or crisis follows. This leads to a host of other needs which arise and cry out for change. This was evident because by 1780 the religious climate reverted back to the conditions before 1725. This was also apparent after 1843, when the Second Coming didn't take place as William Miller and the other millennialists predicted. Because of this over-blown expectation, disappointment and dissatisfaction set in that in turn contributed to the 1858 world-wide revival that followed.

"In Joseph Smith's time there were periodic revivals here and there into the early 1800s which were considered the beginning of the Second Great Awakening. But a significant part of that awakening occurred around 1830. It began in Boston and New York, extending even to the borders of Texas. Later, the area of central and western New York was called the 'burned-over district' because so many revivals had swept through it.

"But like other post-revivalist periods, it found the people tired of the individualism they had reaped. They became spiritually insecure, dissatisfied with the status quo, and found themselves discontented with the cold formalism of the churches.[4] The latter, however, is always an inevitable product of any religious movement. Hoffer mentions it, as does Bernard A. Weisberger in his study of the American revivalists in *They Gathered at the River*. Weisberger states, 'What is conceived in ecstasy must be reduced to form, doctrine, ritual, and organization in order to perpetuate itself.'[5] We'll see this principle prove itself in the Mormon movement as well.

"The people, restless and hungry for truth and a personal experience,[6] were also upset over the inroads of modern thought and the new sciences, especially the Industrial Revolution that challenged their farming habits and shattered their Garden-of-Eden, paradisiacal image of the country. They needed some kind of movement which would maintain the prevailing concept of America as the home for the new Zion.

"As is true in human nature, when people become discontented, they always look for causes outside themselves to solve their problems. In this instance, they felt that to find new purpose and meaning they needed to align themselves with some holy cause. And, as with all holy causes, a new leader is essential. They needed someone, preferably with an authoritarian voice from heaven, to pull it all together for them.

"Everything considered, it was, as Hoffer points out, a critical situation from which they needed to be delivered. And, since dissatisfaction always promotes expectation, these two elements made them ripe for a new religious movement that promised a coming kingdom.[7]

"When people join a movement, they acquire something very important—a new identity. This is no more evident than when new converts are asked to identify themselves. Rather than giving their first and last name as is customary, they give the name of their affiliation: *I'm a Baptist* or *I'm a Lutheran*. It's no different in cults: *I'm a Mormon. I'm a Hare Krishna.* Secondly, they acquire an enduring strength."

"What do you mean?" Elizabeth questioned.

"When a new identity is established, prestige is gained. With prestige comes a power that gives almost supernatural strength to the spirit and soul. This strength can best be illustrated by World War II concentration camps.

"Those in the camps who proved the strongest and most able to bear deprivations were those who identified themselves as members of a party such as the Communists, as priests and ministers of a church, or as members of some 'close-knit national group.' Those who were individualists 'caved in.'[8]

"There are strong psychological needs filled when people belong to a movement: identity, strength, power, purpose, and meaning. And it's my opinion that because a cult fills so many of these needs, that what established Christians often consider a cult's satanic hold on an ex-cultist may actually be the cultist's psychological hold on the cult. The cult member doesn't want to give up all that.

"Now I'm going to give you the principles which the Mormon movement specifically, albeit unconsciously, complied with in order to successfully perpetuate and maintain itself.

"The Mormon Church claims, as do other cults, to have been divinely initiated. But remember stage one? A movement arises, not always because God initiates it, but because there is a culture crisis of some sort where the people look for a change.

"Myra, since you have the book, why don't you read page 103 where Hoffer explains this." Myra quickly flipped through her book. Clearing her voice, she began:

> The leader cannot create the conditions which make the rise of a movement possible. He cannot conjure a movement out of the void. There has to be an eagerness to follow and obey, and an intense dissatisfaction with things as they are, before movement and leader can make their appearance. When conditions are not ripe, the potential leader, no matter how gifted, and his holy cause, no matter how potent, remain without a following.[9]

"Well then," Myra exclaimed, "That means Joseph Smith's movement wasn't successful because God sent an angel with gold plates or because Jesus supposedly appeared to him. It was because the critical situation of nineteenth century America called for a religious movement like Mormonism!"

"Precisely! And if the right conditions don't exist, neither the movement or its leader have any power to sway people to join. But in this instance, the conditions were there, and it led to stage three.

> *Revival:* A restoration of vigor and activity that relieves the crisis situation by offering hope for change.

"But," I said, "even if conditions are right and revival is inevitable, revival cannot be sustained without Hoffer's 'Man of Words' which is stage four.

> *Man of Words arises:* Can be a revolutionary leader, fanatic, or visionary. He gives people what they are hungry for. He does not reform but presents something new.

"Of course, Joseph Smith wasn't the only Man of Words to arise at that time. Do you recall the popular preachers of that period?"

"Yep!" Richard quickly responded. "I remember my history teacher emphasizing the flapping robes of William Miller and his promise of an 1843 millennial reign . . . and Daniel Nash whose voice carried half-a-mile and 'could pray a horse from one pasture into the next.'"[10]

"And," Judy added, "Charles Grandison Finney with his whirling arms and majestic stares."

"You're both right. In addition, there was Lyman Beecher and many others. Revival was going on, which soon led to stage five.

> *People follow.* Joining, they have a preoccupation with unity, self-sacrifice, and a need to identify with something great or eternal—something bigger than themselves.

"They were eager for something—anything—that would unify them and to which they could commit themselves. By embracing what they saw as a holy cause, they found a strengthened life full of purpose and meaning."[11]

Judy interrupted. "It sounds like what you're saying is that the doctrines these 'Men of Words' taught made no difference. Any new concept would have turned the people on."

"Well, yes and no. When people are hungry, it's their concerns they're mainly preoccupied with. But, on the other hand, what a Man of Words proclaims has to reflect the people's needs. Hoffer says that is true with all gifted propagandists, the Man of Words 'brings to a boil ideas and passions already simmering in the minds of his hearers.'[12]

"Joseph Smith knew exactly how to appeal to the people. For example, there was an idea already prevalent about America having a 'manifest destiny.' This greatly influenced Smith's doctrines. In addition, nineteenth-century America already held a national nostalgia for the Adamic concept of America as paradise, the home of the new Jerusalem. These ideas were also reflected in Smith's teachings.

"He also said Christ's coming was near, and they were to prepare America for its change to the new paradise. He claimed that Jackson County, Missouri, was the original Garden of Eden before the continental drift and would be the new Zion, Christ's headquarters. Meanwhile, other preachers were claiming it was Maryland or Georgia. He said those joining his movement would be a chosen people with a promised membership in a ruling elite where they would change the future of the world. Who wouldn't want to be part of that?

"Smith also taught a work ethic borrowed from Jonathan Edwards—'collaboration with God' in a gospel that would fill the whole earth. All of this naturally called for feelings of the most dedicated sacrifice and commitment."

"Mormons today," Judy interrupted, "would be offended if someone said that the beliefs of early American culture had a decisive effect in producing Mormon doctrine. They believe Joseph Smith's revelations came straight from God, having nothing to do with the historical climate. This is certainly interesting."

"Any rising mass movement that is to succeed," I continued, "must offer a close knit organization. This is because people have a passion to belong. In addition, they must also be able to integrate all kinds of converts. In this respect, the Mormon movement appealed to people of many denominational backgrounds.

"To Catholics it offered a hierarchy with an authoritarian head who claimed the power of revelation. To Methodists it offered their own hymns and a system of Bishops. And to 'millennialists and Campbellites [it] offered a new dispensation.'[13]

"In addition, if people were wondering which movement to align themselves with, Smith's amazing pronouncements of angels and contact with heaven confirmed people's unconscious desire of thinking their situation could be solved if only God Himself would speak from heaven. As Catholic sociologist Thomas O'Dea states, it was 'nothing short of a reopening of the heavens to Americans.'"[14]

"You'd think," interjected Melanie, "that he would have turned people off talking about polygamy."

"Smith didn't preach his bizarre beliefs in the beginning," I replied. "Like all fanatical leaders, doctrines like this come later after the adulation of the members is secured.

"But even in the face of strange doctrines, there is an essential ingredient that makes members bond."

"Stage six . . . the presence of a devil!" Myra quickly chimed in. "I'm reading the book," she whispered to the rest.

"Right," I smiled, pleased with her enthusiasm. "This stage plays a crucial role.

> *Necessity for a devil, opposition, or enemy:* Dedication and commitment always thrive best when opposition exists. The leader, therefore, establishes who the enemy is. Opposition acts as a strong uniting factor, promoting a sense of cause.

"'Mass movements can rise and spread without belief in a God,'" I said, quoting Hoffer, "'but never without belief in a devil.'[15] This is because, 'the strength of a mass movement is proportionate to the vividness and tangibility of its devil.'[16]

"Even when Hitler was asked whether he thought the Jew should be destroyed, he answered, 'No . . . we should have then to invent him.' Hitler further explained that 'it is essential to have a tangible enemy, not merely an abstract one.'[17]

"For Mormons," I continued, "the result of having an enemy was unification, cohesion, perseverance, toughness, vitality—and it magnified their cause. Although Mormons try to prove they had an enemy because of the axiom, 'persecution always follows the righteous,' this isn't why persecution came to them. It came because they established an enemy.[18]

"However, it was inevitable they would have an enemy, because new movements usually teach concepts contrary to traditional norms. As time went on, Mormonism's unique doctrines of polygamy, politics, extra-biblical revelation, and members flaunting their eliteness as God's favorites were reason enough to make non-Mormons the enemy. But persecution strengthens, and a good leader knows how to keep this going. Mormon converts bonded together even more closely and were willing to die for their new beliefs, as evidenced in stage seven.

> *Dedication of followers:* Full commitment to one's cause.

"But even though a movement up to this point has all these necessary ingredients, it reaches a stage when the Man of Words has to be replaced.

"This was the case with Smith. Like other Men of Words, he lacked certain attributes to keep the movement going. He could only carry it so far. The movement's continued success would have to depend upon someone else."

"The Man of Action," Myra said.

"Brigham Young!" Judy responded.

"Yes, stage eight."

> *Man of Action arises:* A necessary change if the movement is to survive. He is a man of practicality and law and replaces the Man of Words.[19]

"As Moses was succeeded by Joshua, and Peter was followed by Paul, Joseph Smith was replaced by Brigham Young. I'm not comparing them as spiritual equals, just describing the process.

"Without these Men of Action, movements would probably die. Whether Smith had been murdered or not, Brigham Young, man of practicality and law, was necessary to carry the group to its successful colonization of the West.

"But gradually, after they arrived in the western basin, the principles that originally stimulated them began to diminish. Excitement was dying. This happens to all movements. Brigham, realizing the newness was wearing off and that he could no longer depend upon members' enthusiasm to keep things going, knew he had to do something—and fast. He tried various tactics that led to the next two stages.

> *Institutionalism and hierarchy.* The movement changes from being free and charismatic to a legalistic church. (Stage 9)

Blind obedience and coercion. Force is now necessary to maintain the movement's membership. (Stage 10)

"Mormonism, like early Christianity, entered its institutionalized period and went into bondage under authoritarian dictatorship. Brigham established a legalistic process whereby leaders and members became more subject to him. He depended less and less upon the faith of the members and more and more upon force and coercion. 'Duty was to be prized above devotion.' 'The genuine Man of Action,' Hoffer says, 'is *not* a man of faith, but a man of law.'[20] He must wield a 'sharp sword.'[21]

"With institutionalism, blind obedience, and combining of church and state came fixed boundaries, rigid duties, strict dress standards, legalism, and a squelching of the movement's spirit. There was also a change from a democratic system of voting for leaders to a new system subtly designed to give authorities more power. And, as a typical Man of Action, Brigham saw to it that his new system was accomplished through fear tactics.

"Much like the Inquisition, the Avenging Angels (also called Danites) were organized. It was to this group that the execution of 'Blood Atonement' was delegated. In addition to chasing non-Mormons out of the territory with threats of murder, they kept members fearful of leaving. Mormons who dared oppose the leadership or committed sins such as violating their temple covenants were potential Blood Atonement victims. Brigham Young may have been a tyrant, but without his efforts as the Man of Action, Mormonism would not have survived. That stage brought on stage eleven.

The dark age. The church loses its creativity and freedom and becomes stagnant. Fear reigns.

"One would think the church would have folded, but fortunately for most movements this stage is always followed by a period of rebirth:

Renaissance. Liberation and creativeness. A major change bringing renewal. Legalism, discipline, and blind obedience relax. (Stage 12)

"Often a renaissance occurs because, as Hoffer notes, 'an active movement cripples or stifles the creative spirit.' After a movement ceases its active phase and becomes an institution, there is a 'craving to fill the void left by the lost or deserted holy cause.' Therefore, a 'creative impulse' arises.[22] Like the Christian Renaissance, Mormonism's renewal occurred in the cultural explosion of 1967. The Mormon Arts Festival was inaugurated, creating 'an image of vitality, sensitivity, and vigor.'[23] Their youth began to excel and achieve 'national and international stature in the dance, the theater, music and the graphic arts, painting, the plastic arts, and the literary arts.'[24]

"In addition, higher education was stressed, and members were happy. The church was quite proud of what was taking place and soon acquired a new goal—world acceptance. They expanded their fine arts and concentrated on making contact with leaders of both governments and traditional churches.

"As the hierarchy relaxed its grip, free thinking began to expand. This was no more evident than in two magazines to which Mormon scholars contributed: *Dialogue: A Journal of Mormon Thought,* and *Brigham Young University Studies.*

"Although these magazines gave the cult a new intellectual image, their historians, who were in love with historical integrity, began to expose discrepancies—not with the vigor of anti-Mormon exposés but from an intellectual angle. Not only did the new wave start members thinking for themselves, but the scholarly articles provoked mass inquiry into the church's history and theology. The church's divine claims began to be questioned, and many were beginning to see holes in what had previously been presented to them as facts.

"Members began to suspect a cover up in the church's sacred stories, especially after Utah University professors began to uncover and print suppressed documents from the church's archives.[25] This was like opening Pandora's box. Members began to ponder over what Mormon historian Thomas O'Dea describes as 'the mythology and the stupidities' of Mormonism.[26]

"Historical exposés alone, however, were not responsible for planting the seeds of apostasy. It was because the church was growing weak—it was no longer exerting strong, authoritarian control.

"True to Hoffer's analysis that says a movement will always be successful while it exerts strong control but will lose members when it becomes weak, apostasies increased. This confirms the fact that when members of a cult leave, it is *not* because they want to be free of control, but because they are discontented with the *weaknesses*. When they long to return, it's usually for the *controlled* life.

"Leaders, realizing they needed the kind of influence they had in earlier years, saw the importance of reviving an old principle to guarantee its survival:

> Reinstitution of blind obedience. (Stage 13)

"In this stage leaders planned a careful campaign. Through speeches, sermons, and official publications, they began to emphasize faith over reason. They adamantly opposed Mormon scholars' assertion that 'truth is determined through the intellect and supported by empirical data.' Instead, they declared that 'reason' and its proofs were valid *only* if it confirmed the claims of Mormon revelation. 'The major qualification for the historian of Mormonism . . . [was] conviction, not competence.'[27] Free-thinking scholars, threatened with ex-communication, were pressured to withdraw research papers. They quietly obeyed. Authors who uncovered damaging facts about the early church were banned from speaking at church meetings. The administration at Brigham Young University was 'forbidden to publish in any independent LDS journal or speak at meetings of Mormon intellectuals.'[28] They all complied.

"But the damaging evidence had already been published. To thwart this, leaders began making the following statements to the membership:

> Our individual, personal testimonies are based on the witness of the Spirit, not on any combination or accumulation of historical facts. If we are so grounded, no alteration of historical facts can shake our testimonies.[29]

"Members on the brink who want their doubts eliminated, jumped on the new bandwagon. Reconciling the dissonance of 'fact versus faith,' they said to themselves, *These historical 'facts' which are causing my friends to apostatize are somehow not facts at all. They are, rather, a clever plot of Satan to lead me away from the truth. God is more pleased with blind faith and a testimony that is not swayed by contradictions.*

"The campaign was effective. Things settled down and the Mormon movement began to prosper again.

"But the scholars' intellectual integrity wouldn't let the matter rest. Once more they rose up, and in the wake members began questioning again. Church control had to become stronger.

"In 1993, according to the *Salt Lake Tribune*,[30] a major purge believed headed by Apostle Boyd K. Packer (nicknamed 'Darth Packer')[31] began to acquire information against these dissidents in a 'clandestine manner.'[32] The *Strengthening the Members Committee,* which some members call the church's intelligence agency, were suspected of acquiring 'monitored speeches, writings and activities of those suspected of apostasy'[33] and passing them on to high church officials. Every effort was made to 'cover-up' the fact that the purge was being directed from the 'highest levels of the church.'[34] This led to the actual excommunication of some, including lay members who asked too many questions or stated facts dangerous to the faith of other members. It was a warning to members."

Melanie interrupted. "In view of all this, do you think the Mormon Church will ever die out?"

"No," I replied. "I believe it will continue to survive, not because it had a divine origin or because God is necessarily sustaining it, but because it has and will continue to exert strong control, promote fear in its membership—in other words, utilize all the necessary principles and strategies to successfully get through each stage it encounters. A movement will always prosper *without* God if it

- follows the necessary principles as established in the stages of all successful mass movements,
- changes structure and leadership at crucial points,
- meets the sociological needs of its general membership,
- maintains tight control,
- and makes periodic accommodations to society.

"Movements that do not comply with these principles," I said, "eventually disintegrate."

"What does *periodic accommodation* mean?" Richard asked.

"That means giving up a belief or practice that society frowns upon. The Mormon church's first accommodation was in 1890 when it gave up polygamy and economic separation. In 1978 they appeased the civil rights movement by allowing African-Americans to hold the priesthood. And lastly, they deleted material from the temple ceremony which was offensive to traditional churches.

"Accommodation is crucial for a movement to maintain itself if it wants to survive beyond the first and second generation."

There was silence for a few long seconds. Laying my notes on the table, I studied their faces. Then Judy spoke.

"This is all pretty heavy stuff. But it certainly presents the Mormon Church in a new light—all cult movements for that matter." Turning to Myra, she said, "I want to read Hoffer's book when you and Elizabeth get through."

"I'm going to buy my own book," Richard interjected. "I'm going to study it and note as many applications to ISKCON[35] as I can." Elizabeth declared she was going to do the same for the Unification Church.

Myra gave a deep sigh. "Wow, if I had known all this when I first came out, it sure would have eliminated my hangup over this divine origin thing. I could have saved myself a lot of grief. Too bad more ex-Mormons don't understand this."

I couldn't agree more.

How Can Christians Help?

Inform the cultist about the progressive stages of mass movements. When a former cultist finally understands that his cult's longevity and success is not because of divine origin but because the predictable stages common to all mass movements were successfully handled by leaders, he frees himself from one of the predominant holds the cult has on him. It lessens his longing and feeling of godly obligation to return to the cult.

While the former cultist may not voice aloud his belief that his cult's success is the result of God's endorsement, rest assured he or she is *thinking* it. (It may start out as an unconscious thought at first.) By being aware of the new believer's need to have this problem addressed, Christians can more easily pick up on subtle comments the former cultist may make. And when giving any person information, it is most useful when needed. In other words, there is a right time and a wrong time to present this material. But if it's the right time, have the new convert read this chapter or study Eric Hoffer's book *The True Believer.*

The evening had proved fruitful and apparently was a major turning point for Myra.

"All of this is pretty impressive," Myra said soberly. "It's hard to believe that the Mormon Church's assertion that its success proves God's endorsement bound me to it that much."

"Myra, how do you really feel at this point?" I asked.

"Well," she mused, "I feel different somehow. Seeing the Mormon Church as just another movement throws it into a whole new different light. I don't have that same feeling of obligation to go back. I feel strangely detached like . . . I know, free!"

She hesitated for a few seconds then suddenly blurted out, "John 8:32! I never knew what it meant until now! It says if you *know the truth, the truth will set you free!* That's what's happened! Because I know the truth about what makes a cult prosper—that divine origin has nothing to do with it—I'm free from being tied to it! The Scripture really works!"

Myra was so elated over her new insight, that she asked, "Do you think that it was the Holy Spirit that called that Scripture to my mind? In John 14:26, Jesus said, 'The Holy Spirit, whom the Father will send in my name, will teach you all things.'"

I grinned. "I'm sure of it, Myra."

The remainder of the evening was spent sharing experiences where the truth of God's Word brought them freedom in a particular area.

Convinced that their cults' longevity and prosperity did not prove a divine origin eliminated a major problem for the group. However, it did not mean all other problems were dissolved as the next chapter will show.

Chapter 6 Notes

1. A 1993 figure extracted from the Mormon Church's *Church News* section of the *Salt Lake Tribune,* by Utah Missions, Inc., Marlow, Oklahoma.

2. Eric Hoffer, *The True Believer* (A Mentor Book, The New American Library, 4th printing, May l962), Hoffer, preface (no p.n.). Used with permission of HarperCollins Publishers.

3. "'People,' says Hoffer, 'who are not conscious of their individual separateness, as is the case with those who are members of a compact tribe, church, party, et cetera, are not accessible' to this need for change." Ibid., 54.

4. Clifton E. Olmstead, *History of Religion in the United States* (Englewood Cliffs, N.J.: Prentice-Hall, 1960), 334.

5. Bernard A. Weisberger, *They Gathered at the River: The Story of the Great Revivalists and Their Impact upon Religion in America* (Boston: Little, Brown and Company, 1958), 130.

6. Sydney E. Ahlstrom, *A Religious History of the American People* (Garden City, NY: Doubleday & Co., 1975), 575.

7. Ahlstrom, 574.

8. Hoffer, 61.

9. Ibid., 103.

10. Weisberger, 106.

11. See Hoffer, 54.

12. Ibid., 98

13. William J. McNiff, *Heaven on Earth: A Planned Mormon Society* (Oxford, Ohio: Mississippi Valley Pr, 1940), 48-49.

14. Thomas O'Dea, *Sociology and the Study of Religion: Theory, Research, Interpretation* (New York: Basic Books, 1970), l49.

15. Hoffer, 86.

16. Ibid.

17. Ibid., 86. See also Hermann Rauschning, *Hitler Speaks* (New York: G. P. Putnam's Sons, 1940), 234.

18. Ibid., 86.

19. Ibid., 136.

20. Ibid. (Italics mine)

21. Ibid., 98.

22. Ibid., 140.

23. Leonard J. Arrington, "Views From Within and Without," *Brigham Young University Studies*, W74, 14:141.

24. Ibid.

25. "Crisis in LDS History," Utah Lighthouse Ministry, Salt Lake City, Utah, *Salt Lake City Messenger*, January l986, No.59, 33.

26. Thomas O'Dea, *The Mormons* (Chicago: University of Chicago, 1957), 237.

27. James L. Clayton, Dean of the Graduate School of the University of Utah,

"On the Different World of Utah," *Vital Speeches of the Day,* n.d.: 190.

28. *The Inner Circle,* (Marlow, OK: Utah Missions, June 1986), No. 6, vol. 3.
29. "Crisis in LDS History," *Messenger,* January 1986, 59:33.
30. "Mormon Inquistion?", *Salt Lake City Messenger,* Utah Lighthouse Ministry, Novermber 1993, 85:8, 9. See also *The Mormon Purge* by Jerald and Sandra Tanner, available from Utah Lighthouse Ministry, P.O. Box 1884, Salt Lake City, UT 84110.
31. Ibid., 85:9.
32. Ibid., 85:8.
33. Ibid., 85:6.
34. Ibid., 85:8.
35. International Society for Krishna Consciousness.

7

RITUAL

*Examining the convert's
loss of religious ceremony*

I'm not talking about having my throat slit from ear to ear," Linda stated. "What I'm saying is, I miss the *good* part of ritual."

My daughter and I were watching the Olympic games. We thrilled as we witnessed dazzling fireworks erupting against night skies, brilliant banners, the transporting of the torch, and lighting of the symbolic flame. We were also stirred at the closing with the solemn presentation of flags, teams exemplifying the universal brotherhood of athletes, the celebration of achievement, and a unified crowd's mystical identification with the roots and rituals of the Games.

Linda was quiet for what seemed a long time. Finally, she said, "They really know how to do it up good, don't they? I mean, how could they begin the games without lighting the flame? And how could they end it without all that solemn ceremony? It just wouldn't make you feel that something grand and glorious had just taken place. People would go away feeling cheated, like something was left undone. It would be like hearing Handel's 'Hallelujah Chorus' sung but stopping just short of the final hallelujah."

"Yes," I replied, as I got up and turned the TV off, "what they've presented is powerful ritual—ritual the human spirit seems to demand. And I suppose," I said jokingly, "if someone happened to turn on TV and catch these last exercises and didn't know it was the Olympics, they might think it was a religious ceremony."

Linda was quiet again.

I turned and faced Linda. "What are you really talking about?" I asked curiously.

"I don't know how to say this without it sounding like I miss Mormonism—because I don't miss it at all. But I think I miss ritual. I miss the feeling of entering a sacred place where I can consecrate and give my whole self to God. Of course, I'm not talking about the objectionable parts in the Mormon temple ceremony, like having your throat slit from ear to ear if you reveal passwords.

"What I miss about the Mormon temple is being in another dimension as opposed to this one. Men and women in white robes speaking in hushed whispers, having holy garments placed on you, being anointed with oil, receiving a new name, kneeling at altars, and through covenants and sacred tokens, promising to live the Law of Sacrifice, Obedience, Chastity, and Consecration. Mom, I was willing to give everything I had to God!"

"I know," I replied gently.

"Maybe if I'd never taken part in a religious ceremony, I wouldn't miss it so much. But since I have . . . well, the closest my church gets to ritual," she continued, "is when the choir marches down the aisle at the opening and closing of service— and I love it! Even that little bit makes something special happen inside me. It effects a kind of response within me. My soul comes to immediate attention—my spirit swells—it feels important and right. But, of course, I'm satisfied with that. I have to be."

I understood what Linda was saying. Ritual occupies a

unique place in religion. While some Christian churches do provide ritual, many don't. But it is through ritual that a religion expresses its unique meaning. It is through ritual that sacred stories are reinforced, member-commitment is strengthened, rites of passage are gained, and identity with the community is established. And it is through ritual that consecration to one's God is affirmed.

While not all ex-cultists miss ritual, some do. For the latter it is a loss felt after they develop a strong commitment to their new faith and find they have no way to express it ceremonially. As a result, a former cultist feels unfulfilled and at loose ends in her church in the areas of worship, relationship to God, and identity with the Christian community. The new believer senses something is missing and soon finds himself longing for cult ritual.

Richard's longing for ceremony was evident after he described the *arti ka*, a ritual for new recruits in the Hare Krishnas.

"There was just something about the flickering lights, pounding drums, and the feverish jumping dance," he exclaimed. "Believe me, it was an intense experience. And the incense! I felt I was participating in something ancient, known only to the masters. Of course, I no longer believe in ISKCON or Bhaktivedanta, but I miss how ritual made me feel.

"Do you think," he asked seriously, "my longing for religious ceremony is just a carry-over from the cult's programming? Or do you think it's God-implanted?"

"Good question," I mused. "But your need for ritual could also be the result of hereditary customs passed down in your genes by thousands of years of preceding generations. However, if it is God-implanted, it would suggest that God expects man to appease that instinct. Of course prayer is probably the kind of ritual He had in mind—but, then, prayer can take on many forms."

"If," Richard declared somewhat excitedly, "it is God-implanted, perhaps ritual started because men had to respond to this divinely implanted need to seek God. While they may not have known the true God, should an outsider condemn their ceremonial attempts? Shouldn't one look, rather, at their motive and the inward need they're responding to?"

"Richard," I said seriously, "is this all stemming from your need to justify your participation in Krishna rituals?"

"Well, maybe it is," he said haltingly. "And while I'm certainly not saying our ceremonies were Christian, nevertheless, I think I have a valid question."

"Why don't we get everyone else's opinion," I suggested. "Are you still planning on the picnic Saturday?"

"Wouldn't miss it!" Richard grinned.

It was a warm, sunny day. We all piled into my van and headed for the park. Choosing an old redwood table beneath a giant eucalyptus, we spread our table cloth and potluck. As we did, I briefly described to the others how the closing exercises of the Olympic Games affected Linda.

"Well," Elizabeth grinned, "I believe some ritual is important, but I don't think it makes much sense to jump up and down on a street corner all day, chanting 'Hairy' Krishna, when you're already bald-headed." She leaned over and patted Richard on the arm. "I'm really saying this in fun." Richard nodded.

"Now, you take my ceremony," Elizabeth continued. "We'd sit before a table containing a bowl of flowers and a picture of Sun Myung Moon, bow three times to the Heavenly Father, meaning Reverend Moon, and then to him and his wife as the true parents. Then we repeated a pledge in unison, recommitting ourselves to the Unification Church."[1] She added, "Please note that it's not worship of Reverend Moon, but the pledge I'm emphasizing: *I will fight with my life. I will be responsible for accomplishing my duty and mission. This I pledge and swear; this I pledge and swear; this I pledge and swear.*[2] It still affects me, just saying it."

"The reason," Richard interrupted, "you think your ritual expresses greater commitment is because you don't know anything about mine. Do you know *why* I chanted that mantra as many as 1000 times a day? That took a lot of discipline!"[3]

"No," Elizabeth shook her head.

"First," he continued, "it was a way to get in touch with my transcendental consciousness. By transforming myself, I'd bring about a change of heart in everyone else. I believed when outsiders heard me chant that powerful mantra, it would really change them. While I know now that it had no power, I at least believed I was doing something to change the world!"[4]

"C'mon you guys," I laughed, shoving a dish of baked beans between them. "This isn't supposed to be a contest of 'my cult ritual was better than yours.'

"However," I continued, "whether you know it or not, Elizabeth has discovered one of the reasons why ritual is so powerful. Ritual is more than a physical action; it's the public verbalization of a vow—a do-or-die commitment that gives purpose. The bowing and other motions simply confirm the pledge and give the words more power."

I quickly glanced at Judy who was popping a deviled egg into her mouth. "As far as missing ritual," I said, "I guess Judy is the exception in our group."

"Well," Judy replied, quickly washing down the egg with some Kool-Aid, "I haven't made any bones about how I feel about the Mormon ceremony. The first time I entered the Temple after being taught that ritual in other churches was wrong and that God wanted simplicity, I was shocked. What a contradiction!

"There we were, all dressed alike, performing ritual, giving handshakes, taking our robes off, putting them back on, first on one shoulder, then the other, vowing to have our stomachs ripped open if we revealed any of it. It completely turned me off. However," she admitted, "I do think that when I swore to keep the law of chastity and consecrate all I had to the building up of the Kingdom of God, that part made me feel good."

"Well," Melanie quickly interrupted, "it was the joy of my life to enter the Mormon temple. It thrilled me to think God expected me to give everything I had to Him, including my life. Actually, I think the violence of the death oaths passed over my head. I was so enthralled, believing I was participating in a ceremony supposedly received from heaven, that I didn't pay much attention to the rest. But, what really appealed to me was entering a supposedly sacred place."

"How many of you," I asked them point blank, "miss ritual—I don't mean the cult or its doctrines, but ritual for its own sake?"

"I do," Elizabeth said hesitantly. "I admit I like the idea of participating in a ceremony where I give my all to God. In my present church, aside from a once-a-month communion service, the only ritual we have is the occasional dedication of a baby."

"How does that ceremony make you feel?" I asked.

"Well, as I watch it I say to myself, it's a wonderful tradition to ask God's blessing on a baby. However, it is not *my* baby, so how do I personally relate to the ceremony? How does that ritual put me in touch with God? It doesn't—not in the way I'd like. But I do have to add that once-a-month communion services definitely affect me."

"So, what you're really saying," Richard said, "is that there's something deep within you that cries out for ritual."

"Whoa, Richard," I interrupted. "We don't know whether this need is God-implanted or not. But hopefully we can arrive at some answers that may help some of you to quit thinking about the cult.

"Here's something to consider," I continued. "It's something Melanie touched on. Besides the verbal pledges and the physical motions that empower them, your desire may simply be a need to enter *sacred space.*

"Sacred space," I explained, "is made such by its sacred objects, symbols, and decor. Ask an Episcopalian or Catholic their feelings when they enter their sanctuary with its red, blue, and purple stained glass windows, golden vessels, lampstands, the procession of high mass, incense, kneeling to receive the sacred wafer."

"I relate to that," Richard commented. "The incense in my temple made me feel something special was taking place."

"Yes, it does something to one's soul. I think Joseph Martos gave the best explanation of sacred space when he said it 'is experientially different from ordinary space.' Meaning that when one is in a special place, whether it's a national or religious shrine, the 'space' is 'charged with significance.'"[5]

"Maybe that's why," Melanie spoke up, "I was more caught up with entering a Mormon temple than the ceremony itself."

"So," I continued, "maybe what we're really talking about is not missing ritual, but missing the feelings that arise as the result of being in this special atmosphere."

"But," Judy interrupted, "although I know all that affects a person, I still have to ask this question. How do physical objects or stained glass windows have the power to do that? Is it by believing they are indeed sacred, that it activates some spiritual center within us?"

"That's it," I replied. "Neither things nor places have sacred power in and of themselves, so it's something we project onto them. The cross, for instance, may be just two pieces of wood, but knowing Jesus died on it for us charges it with significance. Thomas Merton said that a symbol 'aims not at communication but at communion.'[6] And the latter takes place when the sacred center of one's soul is touched. The amazing part is the principle works the same for members of any religion.

"Symbols," I explained, "while they can be anything one chooses—a rock, a rosary, even a particular Scripture—become so deeply embedded in a person's soul that it takes a long time to undo conditioned responses and become immune to them. They also act as a trigger. A former cultist can be observing a Christian symbol or hear a specific Scripture and suddenly be tuned back into the cult."

"I had that happen!" Myra said. "I was in church and the Pastor quoted Isaiah 29:11 about the sealed book. All I could think of was the cult's interpretation of it. As a result, a picture of the *Book of Mormon* immediately came into my mind. But what overwhelmed me was the effect it had on me! The experience called up such depths of spiritual feelings and emotions that it was like a confirmation from God telling me the cult's use of that Scripture was true and that the *Book of Mormon* was true."

"No, Myra," I quickly said. "Let me tell you what was happening. I remember when this used to happen to me, and I've come up with an answer.

"When an ex-cultist observes or hears something which triggers a cult symbol, in your case the *Book of Mormon*, the symbol has power to call up former feelings of personal devotion to God. It was your former devotion, Myra, not any truth about the cult or the *Book of Mormon* that touched your inner core so deeply.

"Sometimes, the emotions are so strong," I added, "it can reduce one to tears of homesickness. But, it's not homesickness for the cult itself but for the intensity of one's former dedication. The reason you think it's homesickness for the cult is because that's the *environment* where you experienced all your personal devotion. Because of this powerful effect, the symbol appears to *confirm* the cult.

"What you must remember is that a symbol never conveys information or truth about anything. An object in and of itself is neutral. You are the one who applies meaning and significance to it. All a symbol does is direct man to the sacred center within himself. This is confirmed in Ecclesiastes 3:11 where it says God 'has also set eternity in the hearts of men.' It is this center within you which was responding and reverberating. You mistakenly interpreted it as a confirmation, but your feelings had nothing to do with the cult itself."

"I wonder," Judy said quietly, "considering a cult has more symbols than Christianity does, if that could be the reason the cult has such a hold on us? I've only been able to list four Christian symbols: the cross, the dove, wine, the Bible, and a few key Scriptures."

"Well, you may be right. According to theologians, churches and cults that offer more symbols are able to move their membership into a deeper spirituality. And cults take full advantage of symbols, knowing they produce dynamics that appeal to the deep feelings of the unconscious. There's some kind of throb of resonance within," I explained, "that responds to a symbol. It's like two musical strings that are tuned exactly alike, and one automatically vibrates when the other is plucked."

"It would be interesting to know," Judy said, "what really takes place inside us when this happens."

"Judy," I laughed, "if there were a scientific way to explain it, I'm sure you would be the first one to figure it out. But for now, let's cut the watermelon."

After handing everyone a large slice, with a side order of Melanie's German chocolate cake, Richard shifted the subject.

"Here's something that's puzzling," he said. "There was just something about my temple that affected me but had nothing to do with sacred objects. Somehow the building itself had some tie to antiquity plus a mystical link with heaven. How the cult achieved this, I don't know. But I rather imagine other cult temples effect the same feeling."

"Let me give you a little history," I interrupted. "The ideas you're expressing, about sacred buildings having a link with heaven and antiquity, is something that's deliberately promoted. But let me back up.

"In ancient times, when sacred groves were replaced by

buildings, their location was always the original spot where either the tribe began or where special revelation had taken place. It was known as *the sacred spot which would always remain in union with God.*[7] This concept, with some variation, has been carried down to today.

"It can be seen in Mecca where Gabriel supposedly spoke to Mohammed; in Rome, the two-thousand-year-old center of Catholic Christian roots; in Banaras, India's City of Light and domain of Lord Siva; on the Temple Mount in Jerusalem where Abraham sacrificed Isaac; and in the temple in Salt Lake City where the Mormon Prophet receives his revelation. This is why Moslems are drawn to Mecca, Catholics to Rome, Jews to Jerusalem, Hindus to Banares, and Mormons to Salt Lake City. By pilgrimages and worshiping at these places, people remain in mystical union with the land, their founding ancestors, and their God. But, more importantly, by touching base with these centers, their own sacred centers are affected.[8]

"This is why religious buildings or temples are charged with significance and why ritual within their walls is so meaningful. Followers believe it is where the deity of their particular culture communicates with his people."

"How does the Mormon temple accomplish this?" Melanie asked.

"P.R. work," Judy jumped in. "Melanie, you've just forgotten how these concepts are instilled. The church teaches members that the blueprints for the Temple were given to the Mormon Prophet by divine revelation—just like the plans for the Tabernacle were given to Moses.[9] In addition, the plans were supposed to be patterned not only after Solomon's Temple but also heaven's structure. This establishes the link to both antiquity and heaven."

"That's good, Judy," I said, "but there's even more to holy architecture than that," I added. "Pagan temples of old, besides claiming their building's construction resembled heaven, also maintained that the arrangement of their rooms reflected the number of heavens.[10] This was not an uncommon belief. Some of the apocalyptic writings of the New Testament period name twenty-two heavens."[11]

"Sounds just like the three degrees of heaven depicted in the Telestial, Terrestrial, and Celestial rooms in the Mormon

Temple," Melanie said. "I didn't know they were simply copying what's always been done."

"Yes, and the object of pagan ritual was to advance and gain secret knowledge to enable one to enter those various heavens. Each room acted as an incentive.[12] Armed with secret passwords, one could, at death, ascend from heaven to heaven and pass demons and angels who stand as guards.[13]

"Most of today's cults," I said, "incorporate the same principles popular in the mystery religions during the Hellenistic and Christian era. The Church Universal Triumphant has progressive levels to bring members into communication with Ascended Masters.[14] Followers of Eckankar have ten levels of advancement, and so do many others.[15] Mormon author Thomas O'Dea says it makes the member feel he's 'a privileged sharer in holy mysteries.'[16] In addition, part of the secret knowledge was receiving a new name. This was also an old belief mentioned in ancient texts as well as the Book of Revelation. It's certainly a common practice among today's cults."

"Why, that's right!" Elizabeth exclaimed "After I burned the list of my sins, I was given a new name too!"[17]

"Temple Mormons follow the same pattern," I said. "It invokes a mystical feeling."

"To be totally honest," Judy said, "I think the concept of progressive knowledge could be listed as one of my more serious losses. When I first entered a Christian church and discovered there were no levels for spiritual advancement, I felt my growth was stunted—like I had reverted to a kindergarten level. I wanted to gain higher knowledge, learn godly secrets! I was lost without that incentive! I really expected Christians to have inner circles that would provide this. I thought that if Christianity is the truth, it should have more secret knowledge to offer than Mormonism." She sighed. "I guess I'm just a Gnostic at heart!"

As we all continued eating our picnic lunch and chatting about what each felt was the most difficult part of religious ceremony to give up, Myra reminded us of something we forgot.

"We've talked about symbols, sacred space, and temple architecture. But where does the actual performance of ritual fit in? I know you said it confirms and empowers the pledges, but does the physical movement itself also trigger a person's spiritual center?"

"It's all interconnected," I answered. "The physical motions have two powerful purposes. "First, to tie sacred place, sacred space, sacred symbols, and sacred architecture all into one neat bundle. Second, to confirm and authenticate doctrines, beliefs, myths, pledges, or whatever goes to make up the cult's beliefs.

"But, we don't want to narrow ritual down to just cults. Ritual is very effective, whether it's part of the Olympic games, cult ceremonies, or Christian communion."

"I recall an event in my church," Richard said, "which at the time I didn't think of as ritual, but I guess it was. It had a powerful impact.

"Our church and another church decided to merge. To celebrate this 'marriage,' they had a mock wedding in every detail—even to the staff as wedding participants walking down the aisle.

"Near the end of the ceremony the two pastors solemnly walked up to a table in front. Two small candles were sitting at each end to represent the two individual churches. There was a larger, unlit candle in the center representing the one church they were to become.

"The church hushed as each pastor lit their wick from the two small candles. Then they both touched their flames in unison to the wick of the large candle. At the very moment their two flames became one, music broke out. The two pastors hugged and the congregation nearly came apart. We sang, we cried, and we shouted. The ritual and symbolism of the marriage and the candles touched us in a way nothing else could."

"That cinches it," Judy decided. "The need for ritual must be inborn. It can't be cult programming because it appeals to all people."

"Sounds like it," I replied, "but we still don't know if it's inborn because of tendencies inherited or handed down from our forefathers or because God put it there. Since we can't know for sure, have we gained anything?"

"I'll tell you what I've gained," Elizabeth announced. "It's helped me realize that my longing for cult ceremony has nothing to do with the cult or its doctrines. Instead, it was for the feelings of dedication and consecration cult ritual invoked within me."

"This has been fascinating," Judy said, as she began clearing up the table. "I guess for me the part of Mormon ritual I miss most is the part which promises knowledge by advancing to higher levels. But I don't think it was knowledge for knowledge's sake. It was because I loved God and heaven so much that I wanted to know everything there was to know about God— move as close to Him as I could. I wonder if this is what the ancient pagans felt about their own gods?"

"Well, as for me," Richard began, "by knowing the gimmicks ancient religions and cults use to make their temples linked with heaven, it takes away a lot of the mysticism I felt. Guess there wasn't really anything special about the incense and the drums. Nevertheless, after listening to what we've discussed, I still believe God instilled the need for ritualistic worship—as long as it's acknowledging Him as the true God. In a way, it's too bad we were in a cult because being exposed to what ritual can invoke within us makes us sense the loss even more deeply."

At that moment the sky darkened and a strong breeze swept through the park. "I smell rain," Elizabeth warned. Hurriedly gathering our leftovers and stuffing our paper plates in a nearby trash can, we headed for the van. As we pulled out of the park, the first drops were splashing on the windshield.

As I listened to their laughing and chatting on the way home, I wondered if their new understanding of how their own cult capitalized on the use of ancient ceremony and symbols would help them get over their longing. I also wondered if Judy, so used to inner circles of advancement, could be content in Christianity without it. I wondered if I was even helping them. But then I remembered those who labored with me— they probably wondered the same thing. I thanked God for their perseverance.

How Can Christians Help?

1. *Practice understanding and love.* While not all former cultists miss ritual, acquiring understanding allows one to see that with those who do, it does not necessarily mean the new

convert wants to return to cult beliefs. Rather, it is simply a longing to ritually express one's dedication to God. George S. Worgul confirms the need for ritual by saying it "is not an indifferent or non-essential ingredient to human life. It is at the basis of what it means to be human."[18]

Although cult ritual may be objectionable to some, it is important to understand that as a sacrament it was as meaningful to the ex-cultist as communion is to the Christian. When a temple Mormon goes through the motions of having his or her throat slit from ear to ear if certain passwords are revealed, the attitude is that they are willing to give their life for whatever God requires. Richard's ritual of chanting was not meaningless. He wanted to change the world. To truly love an ex-cultist in Christ is to also understand him.

When the former cultist senses the Christian understands, it invites him to open up more. Many former cultists refuse to share for fear of censure.

2. *Explain the power of symbols.* An observed symbol in a Christian church, whether object or Scripture, may have traditional connotations for the Christian, but for the new convert it may act as a trigger to the cult. This effects powerful emotions, often misinterpreted as God confirming the cult.

Explain to the former cult member that a symbol does not convey information or truth about anything. A symbol only has power given it by the individual who is observing it. The aroused spiritual feelings are not confirmations about the cult coming from God but feelings from within himself. His own spiritual center is "remembering" his former devotion—a devotion that is personal, irrespective of the cult's theology about God. Since the new convert may not have had time yet to reach the same level of devotion in Christianity, his sense of "homesickness" is understandable.

However, besides producing a good feeling, a symbol can also effect a negative feeling. If this is the case, it is not uncommon for a former cultist to go into sudden and deep depression. The new believer may get up and walk out of church. Go after him and pray for him. Many testimonies have been given about depression miraculously lifting after someone prayed for them.

3. *Consider ritual substitutes.* Since ritual involves physical activity, verbalization, and opportunity for dedication and commitment, substitutes must do the same.

Therefore, one substitute for ritual can be giving one's personal testimony. (This is effective, not only for new converts, but also for established Christians.)

There are two reasons it will help the ex-cultist. First, verbalizing one's new faith in Christ effects a deeper belief. Vincent Herr in his book *Religious Psychology* says, it "focus[es] attention upon the idea," bringing with it "an acceptance of the truth contained in the proposition."[19] The ritual of standing up publicly enforces it. This should be done in a meeting designed for this where the whole membership has the same opportunity. The new convert needs to hear other Christians testify also. (This is not to be confused with asking the ex-cultist to testify about his cult experience. See chapter 10.)

Another reason for personal testimony is that it aids in undoing the cult's programmed testimony. Cults have long been aware of how powerful this particular ritual is and have deliberately incorporated it. The Mormon, for example, has been taught from toddlerhood to give the standard adult testimony: "I know beyond a shadow of a doubt that Joseph Smith was a true prophet—I know the *Book of Mormon* is true, that this is the only true Church," etc. One needs to hear oneself declare comparable statements about his or her new faith.

The next substitute for ritual is service. The ex-cultist often feels a letdown when there is nothing that demands the same kind of sacrificial service as in the cult. He is used to dedicating his whole life to his faith. He needs to be offered an avenue to fill this need. Mental assent to one's new faith alone is not enough. This is not, however, a need when he first defects from his cult, as there is a certain amount of healing which must take place first. (See chapter 10.)

For ex-cultists who miss the enticement of higher knowledge via ritual ceremonies, study and access to informative Christian books may prove a good substitute. At least it helped Judy.

By the time we arrived home from the picnic, the group concluded that ritual, along with symbols, was intended by God to express the inexpressible—otherwise why did it work so well? But, in the same breath, they were also indecisive as to whether ritual was an archaic practice that solely belonged to primitive periods. If not, is it still valid for today?

"I believe God doesn't mind some ritual," I said. "After all, communion is a ritual—so are baptisms, weddings, and funerals. They serve an important function. However, perhaps a fixation on excessive ritual, like the cult's, might be considered too much. It should also go without saying, that ritual must be directed toward the true God.

"But," I continued, "whether any of you are at that level or not, I believe God wants you to go forward however the Spirit leads. Look how He led His people forward from Old Testament ritual. While the old Patriarchs found meaning in temple ritual, animal sacrifices, material garments, and physical circumcision, the converted Jew of the New Testament moved on from there. He left animal slaughter to revere Jesus as the sacrificial Lamb. He put on garments of righteousness instead of linen. And he gave up physical circumcision for circumcision of the heart."

"You're right," Judy decided. "Israel's level of ritual was only intended by God to act as a schoolmaster to bring them to Christ. God said there was no purpose to multitudes of sacrifices,[20] and that all the old rituals are a burden to Him.[21]

"I believe," Judy continued, "that God is leading us out of that level into a new one. Now, don't misunderstand. Even though Christ-centered ritual is valid—after all, we don't want to throw out the baby with the bath water—I think that as new converts God wants us to advance toward higher plateaus of spiritual understanding. For us, it probably means learning more about worshiping in spirit and truth."

"That's great, Judy," I said, impressed. "Do you think this new understanding will help all of you to overcome your longing for cult ritual? Do you think you can find substitutes in the church?"

Elizabeth spoke first. "I think my need for ceremonial commitment can be fulfilled through more active service. Maybe," she laughed, "I'm just going to have to learn to volunteer. I also feel my church should have time for testimony sharing. I know that when I share, as well as hear other Christians, it really strengthens me."

Myra added her comments. "Now I know a sacred object has no power in itself except what I give to it or have been programmed to bring to it. When I see something in Christianity that reminds me of a cult symbol, I'll know it isn't God giving me a confirmation that the cult is true."

Judy sighed. "It seems that most of my problems always end up with study as the solution. But if plowing through reference books and seeking deeper levels of meaning in the Scriptures can replace my desire for extra knowledge, so be it."

As the van rounded the corner to my street, I prayed, *Lord, don't let any in this group go back!* Then suddenly the Spirit forcefully called up Romans 8:28: *In all things God works for the good of those who love him, who have been called according to his purpose.* My heart leaped! God wasn't going to desert them! He brought them out with the purpose of saving them! Richard, Judy, Myra, Melanie, and Elizabeth, even though troubled with problems, were called and predestined to be conformed to the likeness of His Son! I spontaneously broke out in song and the others enthusiastically joined in:

> I'm a new creation, I'm a brand new man!
> All things are passed away, I've been born again.
> More than a conqueror, that's who I am.
> I'm a new creation, I'm a brand new man!

Chapter 7 Notes

1. John Butterworth, *Cults and New Faiths* (Elgin, IL: David C. Cook Pub. Co., 1981), 31.
2. *Life With the Moonies*, T-4. Also, Steve Kemperman, *Lord of the Second Advent* (Ventura, CA: Regal Books, 1981), 82–83.
3. "Cults in America and Public Policy," *Social Issues Resources* (8141 Glades Rd., Boca Raton, Fla 33432), 277.
4. Maurice C. Burrell, *The Challenge of the Cults* (Grand Rapids: Baker Book House, 1984), 119.
5. Joseph Martos, *Doors to the Sacred* (Garden City, NY: Doubleday & Co., 1982), 17. See also Mircea Eliade, *The Sacred and the Profane* (New York: Harcourt, Brace and World, 1959).
6. Thomas Merton, *Love and Living,* ed. Naomi Burton Stone and Patrick Hart (New York: Farrar, Straas, Giroux, 1979), 68.
7. See Mircea Eliade, *Patterns in Comparative Religion* , trans. Rosemary Sheed (New York: World Publishing, 1972), 368–369.

8. Ibid.
9. See Exodus 25 and Hebrews 8:5.
10. See Campbell, *The Mythic Image* (Princeton University Press, 1974), II.87; and Christopher Rowland, *The Open Heaven: A Study of Apocalyptic (sic) in Judaism and Early Christianity* (New York: Crossroad, 1982), 81. Also Eliade, *Patterns,* 373.
11. Christopher Rowland, *The Open Heaven: A Study of Apocalyptic [sic] in Judaism and Early Christianity* (New York: Crossroad, 1982), 81, 510. Also "The Early Christian Prayer Circle," by Hugh Nibley, Brigham Young University Studies, Fall 1978, 19: 62; Ascension of Isaiah 1:4, 15–17, in R.H. Charles, *Ascension of Isaiah* (London: A. & C. Black, 1900), 143–44. Some Jews worked up to seven heavens, and the Samaritans and Pharisees believed in more.
12. Advancing to higher levels was a concept also among the early Christians, although not a biblical pattern to follow. According to Origen, secret teachings were given on three different levels: "Beginners," the "Progressing," and the "Perfect." Mircea Eliade, *A History of Religious Ideas: From Gautama Buddha to the Triumph of Christianity* (Chicago: University of Chicago Press, 1982), 369. In one particular Mormon Fundamentalist group, there were three levels, each with its corresponding ritual: Aaronic, Melchizedek, and Patriarchal, referring to their belief in three advancing priesthoods.
13. See *Nag Hammadi* texts (28), Hek.R. 17ff; also the *Ascension of Isaiah,* 9:1.
14. Walter Martin, *The New Cults* (Ventura, CA: Vision House, 1983), 217.
15. Butterworth, 15.
16. Thomas O'Dea, *The Mormons* (Chicago: University of Chicago, 1957), 59.
17. Butterworth, 24.
18. George S. Worgul Jr., *From Magic to Metaphor* (New York: Paulist Press, 1980), 67.
19. Vincent Herr, *Religious Psychology* (Staten Island, NY: St. Paul Pub., Alba House, 1965), 81.
20. Isaiah 1:11.
21. Isaiah 1:14.

8

DEADLY DOCTRINES TOUGH TO DIVORCE

*Why ex-cultists are reluctant
to give up sacred stories*

Responding to the urgent knocking at my front door, I was shocked to see Melanie's tear-streaked face.

"I can't handle it!" she blurted out. "You're going to think I'm terrible, but I can't speak in that class tomorrow!"

My heart sank. Invited to teach in a cults class at a local Bible college, I advised the teacher I would bring a few of my ex-cultist friends to testify about what Christ had done in their lives.

"Oh, Melanie!" I exclaimed. "We're all depending on you! What on earth has happened to make you say this?"

Melanie collapsed on the couch, taking a few seconds to compose herself. "I appreciate everything you've done for me," she haltingly began, "but . . . I can't fight it anymore. I'm worn out—I want to go back."

Her words struck terror in my heart. How could she be saying this? How, after coming so far, could she be thinking of anything so calamitous—especially after her determination to become more active in her church?

Sitting down on the couch beside her, I gently said, "Now, Melanie, you know that longing to go back is normal. But it doesn't mean you'd be happy if you did. Tell me what's bothering you."

"If I go to that class I'm going to be expected to denounce the *Book of Mormon.* Christians just don't understand how neat those stories are—and the principles, like King Benjamin's sermon on serving your fellowman, Jesus blessing the little children! Someone's bound to say something about Mormon scripture, and they'll expect me to say how wicked and evil they are—all the stories I loved so much. I just can't! But if I defend them, they'll think I still believe in Mormonism."

Then, as if anticipating my thoughts, she defensively added, "No, I don't believe in them anymore. But," she sobbed, "they're just in me! I can't get them out of my heart—they're impossible to erase. I've either got to resign myself to being forever plagued or else return!"

I nearly forgot the realities of being an ex-cultist, that the norm is up, then down, that it takes time for cult programming to dissipate. I nearly forgot the most effective tool a cult utilizes. Myths. The *Book of Mormon* was replete with them.

A myth, said Aelius Theon in the second century, is "a false account portraying truth."[1] Anciently, this was understood—that the principles were what was important, not the story form that surrounded it. Myths, therefore, were not to be looked upon as fiction, but sacred, meaningful stories which gave believers a reason for living. Their true purpose was to touch the inner depths of man and see him through the pain, tragedy, and sorrows of life. When myths did what they intended, they acquired sacred status. All pagan religions used them, and today's cults are no exception.

In cults, myths are proclaimed in general assemblies, expounded in classes, preached in sermons, sung in hymns, displayed in paintings, portrayed in plays, and declared through personal testimonies. Any creative way that can be conceived of is used to embed them deep within the hearts and minds of members. Despite an ex-cultist's willingness to accept Christianity, engrained in the warp and woof of his life are skillfully implanted myths.

When a former cultist enters a Christian church, he or she is still deeply affected by the principles contained in cult myths and continues to cling to them. When he or she is told too soon and without sensitivity that cult myths are fabrications or of the devil, it is the same as saying the inner securities and faith they engender are also false. It is a severe shock to the whole psyche.

All guidelines, standards, and ethics then come into question. Securities begin to tumble; assurances are swept away. One's whole world comes crashing down amid anguished and conflicting emotions. It is one of the worst devastations that can be suffered, and is totally incomprehensible to someone who has not experienced it.

Established Christians, aware only that the individual has left the cult willingly, may wonder how anyone can be seriously affected over the loss of something that is false. This is because they lack empathy, having never experienced an intense devaluing of their own Biblical stories and beliefs. For them to challenge or depreciate a cult's myths too soon will call forth a defense mechanism that will not leave the new believer open to truth.

Because this chapter will clarify the true nature of sacred stories and their role in religion, the reader may misunderstand and feel it is saying that every aspect of a cult's myths are valid and to be revered as much as the biblical account. This is not so.

The reason for this approach is that it is important for a new convert to have a "way" of looking at his former myths. Unless he can see their true purpose, he will see no value in using Bible stories to replace them.

"Are Mormon myths fact or fiction?" Melanie blurted out. "I've got to have a convincing answer! Most of my friends simply denounce them with no attempt at an explanation. I know you also loved Mormon stories at one time—you know where I'm coming from. I've got to hear something that makes sense!"

"Melanie, I know you no longer believe Mormon doctrine or

the Mormon Church. I know you love Jesus and believe strongly that the Bible is the only Word of God. But I also realize that Mormon stories are still very dear to you.

"Certainly the story of King Benjamin inspires members to serve their fellowman unselfishly. The myth of Moroni's life exemplifies perseverance in the face of hardship and loneliness. The seagull story conveys that God hears and answers prayer. The myth of Joseph Smith's first vision says to Mormons that God is as real today as He was in Bible times.

"But, Melanie, the moving stories of King Benjamin and Moroni don't make the *Book of Mormon* or the gold plates an historical fact. Notice what I pulled out of these stories. Not doctrine, not validation of the Mormon Church, but only principles. It's the principles these myths portray that are true, and this is the reason you can't give up *Book of Mormon* stories. You relate to the universal concepts portrayed in them.

"But, and I don't want you to come unglued over this, the stories themselves never really took place. They did not occur in history. Do you know that nearly 150 years later, no archeological proofs have been found to substantiate the *Book of Mormon*, whereas hundreds have been found for the Bible?"

Melanie gave a deep sigh. "I know the stories didn't really happen."

"But, Melanie, you're saying that with your intellect, not your heart. And this is another reason you can't give them up."

"Maybe so," she replied, "but what confuses me is that I prayed about the *Book of Mormon*—just like Mormon missionaries challenge people to do."

"Melanie," I said, "one hardly needs to pray about the content of the *Book of Mormon*. The principles and doctrines in the book are so scriptural and drawn from orthodox Christianity that the pages fairly shout confirmation. Joseph Smith included the United Presbyterian's Westminster Confession. He chose names influenced by the book of Genesis. More than eighteen chapters of Isaiah are quoted, along with the Ten Commandments and portions from Deuteronomy, Malachi, and other parts of the Old Testament. It also borrows from Matthew, Mark, and Paul's writings, and parallels New Testament stories.[2]

"Where potential converts or even members are wrong is by

making incorrect assumptions. They assume that because they receive confirmation of the truthfulness of the biblical Scriptures and principles contained within the *Book of Mormon* that, therefore, Joseph Smith *must* have been a prophet. From there it escalates—an angel *must* have given it to him. Their mistake is in only praying about the content and assuming the origin by deduction. They take the book's authenticity on faith, rather than researching it out.

"Lastly, and the problem that's really hanging you up, is that like all Mormons you've literalized your myths. Believing every myth actually happened at a specific time, you forget that the only purpose of a myth is to relay a profound story about life.

"Now, take eastern religions. Although full of sacred stories, they'd never dream of literalizing their myths like our western culture does. Their stories of gods and goddesses were never meant to convey real personages seated in heaven. Rather, their gods and goddesses are usually personifications of cosmic energies. Even in Greek mythology you find the sun personified by Apollo and the dawn by Daphne. The myth tells how Apollo chases Daphne because he is in love with her and how she runs away from him. It is only a primitive myth to describe how the sun chases away the dawn. No one ought to derive polytheism from this. The surface story is only supposed to be a vehicle to convey a truth."

"It sounds like you're stating a contradiction," Melanie said. "You say sacred stories are not historical events, but they're true. So are you saying *Book of Mormon* stories are both true and false?"

"Yes. They're true if you understand that 'true' refers to the truths or correct principles that are buried within a story. They're true if they promote philosophical and spiritual inquiry about principles for life. But the surface story is not necessarily true. Neither are the doctrines that cults try to establish from them. Visions, dreams, symbols, images, or angels, which are often incorporated into myths, were never meant to produce doctrines or dogma. According to the biblical pattern, that's not how God works. Those who exaggerate a meaningful message in order to establish doctrines are deceivers. You don't find Christians pulling doctrine from the story of Noah and the ark, even though they accept its historicity.

"So, how does this affect you?" I inquired, eagerly searching her face.

"Well, if I were Judy I would say, that's logical, so that settles it. But down deep, I feel like someone raped and robbed me of something valuable." With that, her voice quivered, and she was once again on the verge of tears.

I spent the next couple of hours talking to her, not only sharing with her the trauma I personally went through, but showing her that by drawing out universal and general truths from Mormon stories, she could then find the same concepts in Biblical stories.

By the time we parted, although still visibly devastated, Melanie expressed a willingness to read the Bible stories I had listed for her. She said she'd make an effort to pull the same truths from them as those contained in *Book of Mormon* stories. She also agreed to come to the college class—but only to sit.

The campus was a hub-bub of excitement. Young people were quickly scurrying between buildings, trying to beat the last bell. Those who had no classes were off in a corner or on a bench reading. At first I longed to be back. Then, remembering the hectic schedules, late night studying, intense cramming, 10:00 p.m. curfews, and the desperate attempt to keep one's bank account out of the red, I decided I was glad it was over. It was their turn now.

I motioned Richard, Judy, Myra, and Elizabeth to the building where we were headed. Melanie was relaxed, knowing she wouldn't have to speak. Dr. Warnel greeted us warmly and ushered us into the classroom where we were observed with intense, but interested looks.

I smiled to myself, observing the variety of different expressions on the students' faces—the ones who, with pens poised, were determined not to miss one single word as it fell from our lips, others who had never seen a cultist before and didn't know what to expect, and those who looked like they were ready to pounce upon us to show us where our cults were wrong.

After a brief introduction, Dr. Warnel turned the time over to us.

"All six of us," I began, "are Christians who love God and firmly believe the Bible to be the Word of God. We are also ex-cultists.

"We know each one of you feel God has called you to Bible college—therefore, you want to know how to witness to an ex-cultist. If that opportunity should ever come, some of you will probably come on like a cyclone, spouting every Scripture you know to prove the cultist wrong . . ." Before I could finish, one student's hand suddenly shot up. His name was Matt.

"God expects us to declare His Word!" he said emphatically. "If a cultist has been involved in a wicked cult, he should be told exactly the way it is! I don't think Christians should be weak in their witness!"

"I admire your zeal," I said, "but which is more important—to feel good about having declared the Word without reservation and probably lose the cultist or become more knowledgeable and through sensitivity and sharing Scriptures which show God's love, win a soul? Which kind of cultist is more open to God's truth? The one who has been challenged so fiercely that his defense mechanisms are up, or the one who is loved into the Kingdom?

"There is a right way and a wrong way to witness," I continued, "and I'll leave some books after class that will give you needed insight [see the appendix for a list of these resources]. However, the kind of witnessing you're referring to isn't what we're here to cover.

"I want to talk to you about the cultist who is seriously investigating Christianity and the one who has already accepted Christ. I want to tell you how that ex-cultist feels about his beliefs, and why the insensitivity of established Christians can make conversion difficult—so difficult that he may return to the cult. Hopefully, as a result of understanding this, you'll know how to witness better.

"We're going to talk mainly about cult myths because these are the most difficult for an ex-cultist to give up.

"Since the beginning of time," I began, "all religions have used sacred stories. The reason they are essential is because, albeit they are composed mostly of fiction, they respond to the inborn drive of all human beings to ask questions about existence. As Christians we're fortunate that ours are factual, historical accounts.

"But in early societies, people needed stories which would answer questions. 'Where did I come from? Why is there something rather than nothing? Why is there evil in the world? What happens to me when I die? What are my duties? What is taboo? What is the purpose of my life? . . . What does the future hold?' [3] Stories had to develop to answer these questions. It makes no difference whether a myth reads like a good novel, a fantastic fairy tale, or is an actual event in history. People need answers about life, and myths or sacred accounts do it best.

"God, understanding this need, revealed the Genesis account to Israel. He answered such questions as: *Why do women have pain in childbirth? How did evil come into the world? Why do men have to work by the sweat of their brow?*

"While Genesis is an accurate account and pagan myths are not, it must be remembered that the importance of both are the truths that are to be drawn from them. The value of the book of Genesis, for example, is not to scientifically figure out how the world was made or why serpents talked back then but to understand why man failed God and how spiritual death can be overcome.

"A sacred story, myth or factual, has a particular function—to present an account about the mystery of life from which one can gain insight, meaning, and purpose. For centuries, various religions never intended anything more from their sacred stories than that. When we discover truths hidden deep within a sacred story, something suddenly resonates within our spirit as truth, and we say, 'Yes, that's what it's really all about.' We then make it the guiding force of our life."

At that point Matt, somewhat more subdued, raised his hand again. "Can you give us an example of some myth in another culture that has this profound meaning you're talking about? It's easy for me to pick out the spiritual meaning from Bible stories, but when I look at the stories of eastern religions, to me all they do is promote polytheism."

Just then Richard jumped to his feet. "I can tell you a good Hindu one!" Everyone laughed. I motioned for him to come up.

"This story," Richard began, "is about the ugly Hindu face of the god Kirttimukha. Even though he's ugly, his name means 'Face of Glory' and it appears over the sanctuary doorways of the god of Yoga and his bride, the goddess of life. Now you might think this myth's purpose is to establish gods and godesses, but it isn't. And while you're listening to this, try to be thinking of a Bible passage which relays the same message—because this is what I was challenged to do.

"The legend goes like this: there was a bold and adventuresome demon who came to challenge the highest of all the gods, the god Shiva. The demon demanded that Shiva hand over his goddess, but Shiva, using his power, created a second demon who was more powerful. He had a head like a lion and was monstrous to behold, and his nature was sheer hunger. Shiva's intent was to have him eat up the first demon.

"Now the first demon knew he was at a disadvantage. So, knowing that if he threw himself upon a god's mercy, a god could do nothing else but protect him, that's exactly what he did. This, then, put Shiva in the predicament of having to defend him from the second demon. It also left the second demon desperate for food to satisfy his hunger.

"Who then shall I eat?" the second demon roared. Shiva answered, "Why don't you eat yourself?" So he proceeded to do exactly that. He started eating his feet, then proceeded up his own body until all that was left was a beautiful, shining, yet ugly, mask-like face.

"Shiva, who had great insight, marveled. Here was a perfect example of life, which always feeds upon itself. Shiva therefore said of the ugly, but shining mask, 'I shall call you "Face of Glory", Kirttimukha. You shall shine above the doors to all my temples. No one who refuses to honor and worship you will come ever to a knowledge of me.'"[4]

Richard grinned. "Why are those who enter the sanctuary supposed to reverently bow down to this image? Why are they to honor and worship this demon who like life, as Shiva observed, ate himself up? Who knows the meaning of this myth?" No one raised their hand.

"The homage to Kirttimukha," Richard began, "is not to establish this god's identity but to pay respect to the deeper aspect of life it represents. The meaning is that life has two sides to it. There are the beautiful aspects, symbolized by Kirttimukha's shining face of glory. But, there is also the monstrous side, portrayed by his ugly face. In addition, life indeed seems to eat itself, meaning that life consists of sorrow, tragedy, pain, and death. But it is the way God made life.

"The message is: no one can understand God until one can accept and reverence the way He created life with both its positive and negative aspects. People can never have a true knowledge of God, unless they quit insisting that they could have created life better by eliminating pain and tragedy. They must see the glory in *both*. Life is, after all, God's creation and must be respected. In this myth lies a great truth although wrapped up in the costume of a different culture. Can anyone think of a Scripture which basically says the same thing?" The class looked stumped.

"Jesus taught the same truth in Matthew 5:45—the rain falls upon the just and the unjust. Jesus is saying, this is the way God made life. Bad things happen to both good people and bad people. And in both the positive and negative sides of this dichotomy of life, we are to 'give thanks in all things' (1 Thess. 5:18), even as Job did. The neat thing is," Richard continued, "I can continue to acknowledge the principles, but I no longer have to be influenced by Hinduism."

Richard then sat down. The class not only enjoyed the story, but their facial expressions indicated they were beginning to understand mythic principles and how meaningful they could be to someone in a different culture.

"Do you think," I began, as I resumed my position at the lectern, "that this myth was intended to make Orientals believe there really was a demon god named Kirttimukha who ate himself up?" They all shook their head. "Of course not, they're too smart for that. Richard, trained in the eastern way of thinking, knows the characters in the myth are fictitious. Therefore, it isn't hard for him to eliminate the story and replace the truth it contains with a Scripture which says the same thing.

"Now with westerners it's a different story—and this is why it is so difficult for ex-cultists to give up their myths. They are taught to literalize them.

"Leaders of western cults use myths with an ulterior motive to accomplish three goals:

"First, to literalize myths so members will believe the characters were actual people and the myths historical events. Members will then be reluctant to renounce them.

"Second, to claim stories were received by revelation so it gives them sacred status.

"Third, to teach members that although general principles may be drawn from the stories, the ultimate truth is to confirm God's sanction of their cult and establish doctrine.

"In addition, cults promote another myth designed to establish the divine calling and anointing of their leader. This usually requires the mythical appearance of some supernatural being to the leader. The most effective myth a cult will produce is the one that boasts the strongest supernatural element. The strongest legitimation, of course, is to have the group started by the same being who created the world or who is close to God, which usually turns out to be Christ or Michael.

"It is important for a religion to do this because there must be some kind of story to legitimize a group's coming into existence as an act of God. Otherwise, there will be no followers. In the case of cults, their myths then act as a *sacred canopy*, to use Peter Berger's term,[5] and the more a sacred canopy can be 'umbrellaed' over a cult or church, the more it can maintain its following and perpetuate itself longer. One would certainly have second thoughts about coming out from underneath that kind of canopy!

"These kinds of myths, however, have strong appeal. Cult leaders can claim as fantastic a story as they like, and people will believe them. It can be an angel named Moroni handing out gold plates, Christ speaking to Reverend Moon, or Joan of Arc visiting Moses David. Individuals not only need to believe but must be able to testify that they have 'truths from God.'

"When an individual believes he belongs to a religion with a sacred origin, he feels secure and protected. This leads to intense dedication. Therefore, cult leaders, recognizing this need, deliberately promote myths.

"Even when cultists leave of their own free will, some don't make it outside the cult because they don't want to let go of their sacred myths. Without them people suffer, as poet Archibald MacLeish writes:

> A world ends when its metaphor has died . . .
> It perishes when those images, though seen,
> No longer mean.[6]

I then sat down, motioning to Elizabeth who shyly moved toward the front of the room. She nervously began to speak. "I'm Elizabeth, an ex-Moonie," she began. "But, I really don't think there is any way I, or any of us, can relay to you what a disabling experience it is to lose the stories that meant so much to us. My whole world literally fell apart. I didn't want to live and seriously thought about suicide.

"I loved Reverend Moon and his wife. It's like when you love someone, then break up, you don't stop loving. For me, it took time. I didn't want to believe that the stories about Rev. Moon's divine calling from Christ weren't true. I really believed that on Easter Sunday in 1936 Christ spoke to him, saying, 'Carry out my unfinished task.' I believed in the voice from heaven which confirmed to him that he would 'be the completer of man's salvation and become the Second Coming of Christ.'[7] I believed Jesus and other saints in paradise revealed the *Divine Principle* to him.[8] I believed he was called to raise up a holy family because Jesus failed.

"In addition, the myths about Moon being imprisoned as a religious martyr, his performance of miracles and supernatural strength were all sacred to me—no less sacred than the stories about Jesus. They inspired me, gave me strength and encouragement.

"Nevertheless, I left because of poor food, deteriorating health, and because I discovered some of the stories didn't jibe with the facts. I ended up wandering into a Christian church.

"Christians have been loving and kind to me in most respects; but, in other ways, they expected too much from me too fast. They had no idea what I was going through. They thought I could easily rip my stories out of me because I accepted Christ. But it's just not that easy. If it hadn't been for the support of our little group, I probably would have quit.

"But I believe I'm over the worst part. I've learned how to draw out the principles contained in my cult stories and find them in the Bible. By continuous reading of the Bible, the Word has washed my mind clean of those stories. I now know that Jesus didn't fail in His mission—He has redeemed me completely. Jesus is the Messiah, not Reverend Moon. Jesus is the final revelation of God so there is no need for a restoration through another religion. The *Bible* is the Word of God, not the

Divine Principle. Jesus is the one who sacrificed His life for me, not Reverend Moon. Jesus didn't need to find someone else to raise a holy family—He already had one!"

Elizabeth took a deep breath and returned to her seat while the class eagerly applauded her.

Glancing at my watch, I noticed that class was close to ending. I motioned to my watch as Judy got up. She nodded. As she came up to the front, I studied the students' faces. It was obvious they were enjoying the presentation. I could also tell from their expressions that they were genuinely trying to feel how it must be to lose sacred stories.

"When I was a young girl," Judy quickly began, "I remember two young missionaries on bicycles talking to my mother. In one breath they declared four major Mormon myths.

"'Ma'am,' they said, 'Our religion is special because both God and Jesus Christ came to earth in the Spring of 1820 and started it. These personages spoke to Joseph Smith which makes him a modern-day prophet like Moses. Through him they restored the same gospel that was established by Jesus before it was corrupted by man. In addition the angel promised in Revelation 14:6 delivered to him a book written on gold plates. This book contained the everlasting gospel as revealed to the ancient inhabitants of America. Our gospel is the same taught by Adam as well as all prophets who functioned in other worlds before this one. We are a special and called church. And we testify that all this is true by the power of the Holy Ghost!'

"There," Judy said, "you not only have myths establishing contact with heaven, anointing of a Bible-like prophet, a restored gospel, a biblical angel, but the spreading of a sacred canopy validating Mormonism. This was the most exciting story I'd ever heard!

"After my mother and I joined, I grew to love everything about Mormonism. It was my life, my breath, my inspiration, my all. And although I can talk about it easily now, don't let this fool you. When I left, I was so messed up emotionally, I thought I was cracking up. Losing sacred myths is a serious matter!

"When I came into a Christian church, I looked for the same sacred canopy. But my Pastor didn't claim a comparable story of being called to the ministry like Joseph Smith—he only claimed a 'still small voice.' Neither was there any marvelous visitation from heaven telling him to start his church.

"I went through many disappointments and often felt like quitting and returning to the Mormon Church. I admit I still miss Mormon myths and wish Christians could tell of more miraculous visitations. But it was the love and joy I kept seeing in the faces of Christians that made me keep coming back. I now know the Bible is the only Word of God and Jesus is the only leader I must put my faith in!"

Myra then got up with five minutes left. "The loss of stories from the *Book of Mormon, Doctrine & Covenants,* and *Pearl of Great Price* affected me because they continually affirmed purpose and meaning for me. All this fell apart when I entered Christianity. But the myth that was the most difficult to relinquish was pre-existence. When it dawned on me that to embrace Christianity I had to give up the idea of pre-existence, every bit of me fought against it. Temple marriage I could give up, even Joseph Smith's first vision, but *never* that!

"I believed I had divine parents who sent me to earth on a mission, and someday I would return to them. This myth gave me security and made me feel loved. It assured me I was important in God's plan and that I had a spiritual kinship to Christ. Nothing could happen to me.

"After finding there was no Christian story that confirmed that I existed before this life, had a mission, or that I had heavenly parents—losing all that left me totally empty with no purpose in life and nothing to motivate me. I cried and paced the floor at night, bewildered. I felt alone because I couldn't talk to Christians about it.

"However, all I needed was time. As a result of praying, studying the Scriptures, gaining a deeper understanding of what Christ did for me, as well as understanding the companionship of the Holy Spirit, I've regained *everything* I need."

There was a loud "Amen" from the back of the classroom. She smiled, left the lectern, and I quickly took her place.

"The reason we've shared all this with you is so that during witnessing, even when you quote Scriptures, you can be more gentle.

"In conclusion, let me say this. Try not to minimize the importance of myths. They have an importance place—

even for us today. We remember the myth of George Washington cutting down the cherry tree which reminds us of honesty. Then there's the midnight ride of Paul Revere to illustrate dedicated patriotism (although it was really Dr. Samuel Prescott who reached Concord with the message), and so on. Christians also have extra-Biblical myths that help to strengthen their commitment such as: 'America is God's special country,' or 'We are the only real Bible-believing church.' Although without historical support, they nevertheless meet important needs in certain Christian circles. Now, the world doesn't come to an end when we discover the cherry tree and other stories are only myths. But, on the other hand, myths pertaining to one's personal faith and beliefs are more serious.

"I know it's not possible for you to totally understand what an ex-cultist experiences, but try to picture how you would feel if you were suddenly convinced that everything you believed was no longer true.

"What if you had never heard of the claims of liberal scholars and for the first time were confronted with them? What if they convinced you that your religious beliefs had no historical validity? What if you believed there never had been any such individual as Moses; that the story of Mount Sinai was a story made up by the Jews to portray God's deliverance; that the Bible is fictitious; Jesus was called Messiah by His followers simply because they were desperate for one; the apostles, disappointed in Jesus' death, made up the whole story of the resurrection, and so on? That school of thought can be pretty convincing. What if you believed them?

"Your whole world would literally come crashing down. No longer would there be a sacred book you could believe was from God. No longer would you have role models from the Bible to emulate. Doubt would enter in as to whether there was even a God. You would not be able to pray. You would have no assurance of salvation. You would not know what to expect after death. You could expect no supernatural help in problems. You would have nothing to put your faith in. You would become angry and bitter, believing you had been deceived. Goals would crumble, and you would sense no more meaning or purpose to life. You might be able to imagine this to a certain degree, but there is no way to fully understand unless you actually go through it.

"I'm having Melanie pass out a sheet to you entitled 'How Can Christians Help?' Please follow along."

How Can Christians Help?

1. *Understand the purpose of myths as used in religious cultures.* Myths do have a valid place. Life would hold too many fears if religions didn't provide them. Without this understanding, established Christians may consider former cultists hopeless when they refuse to give up their sacred stories.

2. *Understand myths as sacred stories.* Rather than categorizing cult myths as "lies," remember they are sacred stories that give meaning to one's life. This understanding does not mean you have to agree with the doctrines cults derive from them nor their sacred status. However, do acknowledge the universal principles a myth may portray.

3. *Explain that myths are not meant to establish doctrines or validate the cult.* A sacred story based upon God's pattern in the Bible was never intended to establish doctrine. Tell the new convert that whether it is a cult myth or factual biblical story, it is designed to speak to the inner man about universal and spiritual principles. The surface story is only a vehicle.

All this is not to suggest that Christians should tell new believers that they can continue to believe in their cult myths forever. It is saying, however, to go slowly. Reiterate the stories of the Bible, and as the Word becomes more established in the new believer's life, old beliefs will gradually fade away, and new beliefs will become stronger.

4. *Be sympathetic and patient.* Letting go of sacred stories has a shattering effect that is difficult for others to comprehend. When a cultist finds out that every aspect of a story is not literally based on an historical event, even if only a partial fabrication, it is putting it mildly to say they become "unglued." They become disoriented, full of anxiety, and feel isolated.

5. *Approach ex-cultists with understanding, love, and patience.* Do not challenge them to the degree that it angers them and

they become defensive. The goal is to keep their minds open to receive truth.

6. *Teach them how to replace their myths.* The solution to the new convert's difficulty is helping him understand what a myth is and is not supposed to do. Explain a myth's purpose. Have the former cultist draw out the spiritual or philosophical meaning from their myths and look for replacements in God's Word, while emphasizing the accuracy of the Biblical account. Unless you emphasize that it is the *principles* that are important, the former cultist will be looking for a similar surface story in the Bible, which of course he is not going to find.

"If," I said in conclusion, "the ex-cultist attends church long enough, maintains contact with established Christians, is allowed to participate, and is not put on the defensive, he will inevitably give up his cult myths."

We lingered after class answering questions, then, after saying our goodbyes, piled into the van. Everyone was in good spirits, even Melanie. I wasn't discouraged about her, for I knew that if a new convert stays in the church long enough, it's a psychological impossibility to continue in contrary beliefs. This is because the constant hearing of the Word and influence of established Christians produces an effect. My task was to make sure she stayed long enough.

As I dropped Melanie off at her house, I didn't expect to notice improvement this soon. Nevertheless, she smiled and said, "The next time you want me to participate, I think I'll be able to do it."

What a change from yesterday! Maybe I was going to see some fruit after all. Galatians 6:9 came to mind: "In due season we shall reap, if we faint not."

Chapter 8 Notes

1. Mircea Eliade, *Myth and Reality,* planned and edited by Ruth Nanda Anshen, translated from the French by Willard R. Task. *World Perspectives,* Vol. 31 (New York: Harper & Row, 1963), 165. Used with permission of HarperCollins Publishers.
2. Jerald and Sandra Tanner, *Mormonism—Shadow or Reality?* (Salt Lake City, UT: Modern Microfilm Co., 1972), 73–74.

3. Sam Keen, "The Stories We Live By," *Psychology Today* (December 1988): 45.
4. Joseph Campbell, *Myths To Live By* (Bantam Books, 1988), 105–106.
5. Peter L. Berger, *The Sacred Canopy* (Garden City, New York: Doubleday & Co., 1969).
6. David Leeming, *Mythology* (New York: Newsweek Books, 1976), 74.
7. Chon Sun Kim, *Rev. Sun Myung Moon* (University Press of America, 1978), 9.
8. Ibid., 44.

9

EXIT FROM THE CULT AND CONTACT WITH A PASTOR

What to expect when it happens

No, Pastor—don't come to my home unless it's after dark! Better yet, I'll come to your place. But I won't be able to park in front of your house because my car might be recognized."

When Pastor Smith told me of this Mormon's shocking statement, he was baffled. "Why all the secrecy? What is she afraid of?"

He and his wife invited me to meet with them after their evening service. Richard had told them of my Mormon background, telling them I would be happy to talk with them. I asked Judy along.

Pastor Smith was a gentle man in his late fifties. He and his wife were anxious for insight into working with Mormons.

"She just appeared on our doorstep one evening," the pastor began. "We've only met with her twice."

"Her name is Beth," the pastor's wife interjected, "a single lady in her early forties and very nice. We try to read the Word with her, but she only wants to talk about Mormonism. She jumps from one Mormon subject to another—most of the time she sounds like she's defending it."

"She'll appear calm one minute," Pastor Smith continued, "then suddenly start crying. She says she questions Mormon beliefs but is then defensive of them. She says she's open to hearing about Jesus, but then she's closed. She wants to investigate Christianity but won't come to church—she says someone might see her car. Why is her behavior so *irrational?*"

His assessment was indeed accurate. When a Mormon or other cult member contacts a pastor for the first time, he or she is a bundle of conflicting emotions. Plagued with unrest, the cult member tries to appear in control. I recalled my own experience when I contacted a pastor. Suspecting Mormon doctrine was false, I hoped I was wrong. Full of questions, I felt guilty. Wanting truth, I defended my beliefs. Believing the Holy Spirit was directing me, I was fearful God would reject me. The reason? What if God really approved of the Mormon Church?—a thought that taunts all ex-cultists.

In addition, cult members believe they are being watched, so they are beset with fear. They know friends, even family, feel it their duty to report them. If they are found out, they will be labeled "apostate." No other word can strike such terror in the heart of a faithful member. It carries all the connotations of everlasting hell, outer darkness, perdition, rejection by God, and for the Mormon, invalidation of one's Temple endowment, loss of priesthood, loss of one's spouse and children in the hereafter, and much more. It's not something to trifle with.

Therefore, one's first steps are fraught with fear—not only fear of being discovered by cult leaders but fear that by investigating Christianity he or she will lose beloved beliefs.

The cultist, therefore, arrives with a defense mechanism already set up. He or she will become argumentative at the slightest innuendo against the cult. Even though thinking about leaving, he is still a cultist and will fight to protect his faith. It matters not that he already has doubts about his cult. It mat-

ters not that he is looking to Christianity for answers. It matters
not that he is the one initiating the meeting. His defense system
prepares for the threat the pastor and the new church pose.
From the perspective of those working with cult members, they
are problematic, complex, unmanageable, resistant, perplexing, incorrigible, and exhausting.

After I explained all this to Pastor Smith, he responded, "No
wonder Beth is messed up. But it's hard to believe," he continued, "that a church would actually have members followed."

"Believe it," I said.

"But do you really know that for a fact?" Mrs. Smith asked.

"Yes," I replied. "Not only from friends whose word I trust,
but from my own experience.

"While I was still active in the mainline church, I was
attending undercover meetings of Fundamentalist Mormons
in Salt Lake City. Word, somehow, always leaked out where the
meetings were to be, and Mormon authorities would arrange
to have someone there to take down the license plate numbers
of all cars within a two block radius. Once identified, members
were called in by their Bishop. Fundamentalists who still
retained their membership in the mainline church, which
included myself, were instructed not to come in their own cars.
Yes, the fear is real.

"But even more fearful than being discovered by leaders of
the mainline church," I continued, "is when one decides to
leave Fundamentalism. Some Fundamentalist leaders believe
that apostasy is outside God's grace, so one must atone with
their own blood. Therefore, during the first three months after
I left, I thought I would be killed. I was afraid to walk by a window at night for fear of being shot. Whether this idea was
actually entertained by the leader, I don't know. But, I know my
fear was real.[1]

"Similarly, Moonies believe other Moonies will pursue
them, or else 'fear the psychic revenge of the spirit world.'[2]
Many ex-cultists, according to Dr. Margaret Singer at the
University of California, get 'unlisted numbers, change their
address, even take other names.'"[3]

Judy spoke. "My biggest fear during my investigation of
Christianity," she said, "was being confronted by my Bishopric.
The chance of being found out was so threatening that I began

a kind of hypocrisy. I decided to play it smart by covering both sides—especially since I hadn't made a final decision about leaving yet. So, besides showing an interest in Christianity, I also gave the impression to Mormon friends and leaders that I was still happy in the Mormon church. I reasoned that if my dissatisfactions with Mormon doctrine ended up not proving valid, or if after investigating Christianity I wasn't satisfied with it, I would still have credibility in the Mormon Church and be able to continue functioning in church positions. Fear," she added, "is a terrible thing to live under."

Judy and I shared experiences for another hour. When we were through, the pastor and his wife asked us if we would come to their home and meet with Beth the following night. However, both Judy and I declined.

"Not at this early stage, Pastor. Right now Beth needs to talk about her concerns and grow secure in your presence. She would only be threatened by strangers. Later, as she progresses, you can ask her if she'd be interested in talking with us."

"Well," Mrs. Smith began, "we certainly need to show her where she's wrong in her beliefs."

"Yes, but let that come in time," I said. "I believe a pastor is wise by not blurting out to cultists that their church or cult is false, satanic, or that they are wrong in their beliefs. Pastors who have been the most successful have simply answered their questions, let them talk about their concerns, shared the Word, given their testimony and, most of all, shown love. Beth will appreciate your respect for her.

"But another reason you need to proceed gently is because lying just below Beth's placid countenance is a strong defense mechanism. She can easily become hostile due to her emotional state. This is not to suggest she will become physically violent. It only means that if her defenses are called into play, it will dead-end any attempt at communication."

Judy suddenly nudged me, "It's getting late," she whispered.

Saying our goodbyes, we agreed to make ourselves available when needed.

Two days later, Judy came over to return a book. Our conversation turned to our meeting with the pastor.

"When I got home that night," Judy began, "I went to bed

and did nothing but dream about my excommunication and exit from Mormonism—what a nightmare! But maybe that was good because I'd almost forgotten all the fear and emotions. I thought it would never dim because it was so traumatic—but that isn't so. It seems the more distance I gain from it, the more I forget how it really was."

"Yes," I said, "I hope I never forget because it would affect my rapport with ex-cultists. However," I added, "I've discovered that many ex-Mormons do forget what it was like.

"Shortly after I converted to Christ, I used to become puzzled listening to Christian-ex-Mormons give talks. They came on so strong, suggesting such attack-like witnessing procedures that I knew would never have worked on me. I wondered if maybe they felt obligated to talk that way to gain other Christians' approval. But then I read Latayne Scott's book *Ex-Mormons: Why We Left*. Listen to this," I reached for the book from my bookshelf and flipped to the epilogue:

> I have noticed that the longer people are away from Mormonism, the more inclined they are to be assertive—even aggressive—in dealing with Mormons. Take, for instance, the no-holds-barred approach of long-time believer Granny Geer who "goes for the jugular," immediately confronting a Mormon with the shockingly sexual implications of his theology before she knows his first name. Contrast that with the repeated cautions of, say, Kevin Bond whose exodus from Mormonism is much more recent and who insists on gentleness in witnessing to Mormons. . . . the longer you are away from Mormonism, the more bold—or even brassy— you become in confronting its errors.[4]

"Well," Judy smiled, "let's keep reminding each other so we don't forget . . ."

Suddenly I glanced at my watch, apologized, and told her I had to leave for a meeting.

"That's all right," she said, grabbing her coat. "Keep me posted about Pastor Smith!"

Two months later I received a call from the pastor's wife.

"Jerry asked me to give you a ring," she said. "We've had quite a few meetings with Beth since we last talked with you. And we're certainly glad you explained her emotional state. It's helped us to be more sympathetic to what she's going through. We even acknowledged to her that we understood the courage it took for her to contact us. She seemed to appreciate that.

"But," she added, "we do need a little more input on why she's so defensive of the cult. In one breath she expresses an interest in Christianity, and in the other breath she defends the Mormon Church. It doesn't make sense."

"Well," I began, "there are at least four reasons why she's doing this.

"First, her pride is at stake. As a faithful Mormon, Beth has been trained to boast that her church has special insight into the mysteries of life that others don't have, plus a restored gospel, modern-day prophet, extra-biblical revelation, and visitations from resurrected beings. She can't let go of that kind of uniqueness.

"Second, her ego is at stake. She's ashamed to admit she might be wrong about her faith. It's a terrible thing to admit you've been duped—it makes one feel stupid. For her to admit she's been wrong is the same as her admitting she's not able to discern truth from error—and she wants to appear spiritually mature to you.

"Third, her whole belief system is at stake. In spite of her doubts about Mormonism, she still cherishes her beliefs because of the faith they instill in her. Something deep within her knows how devastating it will be once she acknowledges Mormonism is false.

"Fourth, her secure and anxiety-free world is at stake. The cult for many years has been like a mother—succoring, counseling, doing her thinking, protecting, providing for her needs. It's threatening to step out of that world."

"Well, that certainly sheds some light," Mrs. Smith mused. "I do hope we're helping her. It's hard to tell—she's so difficult at times. Are you and Judy still willing to come?"

"We sure are. However, be prepared that rather than coming on strong, we'll be low-keyed. Beth needs to hear our testimony about Christ and feel free to ask us questions."

"That's fine," Mrs. Smith responded. "It might be a while yet. Should we tell her anything special about either of you?"

"Yes. It's important that you make us credible within her own frame of reference. That is, tell her what positions we used to hold in the Mormon Church. When a Mormon is going to meet an ex-Mormon, this makes a big difference. Active Mormons won't be impressed by hearing you tell of an ex-Mormon-turned-Christian, *unless* that person held a prominent position in the Mormon Church. This tells them how spiritual he or she was. They'll then value what an ex-Mormon has to say."

We then concluded our conversation with a run-down of Judy's and my former Ward positions.

A few weeks later, Mrs. Smith called to say that Beth had finally resigned from her church positions and had asked to have her name removed from the rolls. "But," she said, "working with her has been like a roller coaster! First her emotions are up, then they're down! Jerry and I have spent a *lot* of time in prayer. It's good we remembered you said it would be like this. We keep saying to ourselves, 'This is normal—this is normal!'"

It was two more months before we finally met Beth. She was very neat in appearance, had brownish-red hair, blue eyes, and was rather timid. It was obvious, however, that she had established a good rapport with Pastor Smith's wife.

"Beth," I said warmly, "I'm so happy to meet you." I shook her hand. "Judy and I are here just in case you'd like to ask questions." She was friendly, but reserved. It was Judy who finally broke through.

"I understand you were very active in your Ward," Judy said. "What job did you hold?"

"I was Primary organist," she replied hesitantly, "and I taught the twelve-year-olds."

"That's what I did too!" Judy exclaimed. "I mean the organist part. I played for both Sunday School and Primary." Beth displayed a big grin, and the ice melted. After that Beth smiled more, giving no indication of having problems.

Mrs. Smith, who had disappeared into the kitchen, called to us. "Come on all of you—I've made some hot chocolate!"

We filed into her neatly arranged kitchen and reached for our cups of steaming cocoa. After plopping some marshmallows in, we sat around the table.

The pastor began by directing his remarks to Judy and me. Although Judy and I were already apprised of Beth's progress, he did it more for her sake than ours. He told us about Beth's dissatisfactions and her questioning of Mormonism, all the time emphasizing that it was the hand of God that had led her.

"Do you believe God brought you here?" I asked, turning to her.

"Yes," Beth replied, "I could never have done this on my own. I only hope," she hesitated, "I've done the right thing. I mean," she added—there was a long pause—"what if Mormonism is really true and God rejects me!" She suddenly turned her head so we couldn't see her face. "I'm so messed up," she continued in a discouraging tone, "but I want the truth ." She began to cry.

"Beth," I said, patting her on the arm, "Judy and I went through exactly the same thing you're going through—we know how difficult it is. But let me tell you—we couldn't have made it if it hadn't been for the Lord and the Christians who stuck with us. You're going to make it because you have the same thing going for you. God has led you to Pastor Smith and his wife, and we're also here for you."

I turned to Psalms 50:15 and began reading. "God said, 'Call upon me in the day of trouble and I will deliver you . . .'"

Suddenly Beth cried out, "I don't know how He can deliver me from what's happening to me!" she exclaimed. "It's wearing me out!"

I glanced at the Smiths, and they shook their heads, indicating this was something new.

"Tell us what's happening," Judy said gently, scooting her chair closer.

"It's sorta hard to explain. But ever since I left the Church, I've been plagued both day and night with 'Mormonism' on my mind. When I wake up during the night, it's there. All day long, it's there. It's 'Mormonism, Mormonism' constantly in my mind driving me crazy! I can't quit thinking about it!

"And it makes no sense because I'm convinced Mormonism is false. But it's just *in* me, and I can't make it leave. How do I get rid of it?"

"Beth," I said, "are you an avid reader?"

"Yes," she said, surprised.

"Do you still have your *Book of Mormon* or any of the writings of Joseph Smith or Brigham Young in your home?"

"Well, yes."

"Listen to me carefully—I have a suggestion that I feel will work—that is, if you really want relief." Reaching for my Bible, I turned to Romans 10:9.

"Beth, there is power in the spoken word because the Bible says so. In Romans it says that if you confess with your mouth that Jesus is Lord and believe in your heart that God raised Him from the dead, you will be saved. Verbalizing is important enough that God repeats it again by saying that it is with your *mouth* that you confess and are saved.

"What I'm saying is this. You need to verbally denounce the writings of Joseph Smith and Brigham Young, and you'll be free of what's plaguing you."

For a fleeting second panic shot over her face. But it left as fast as it came . . . she was good at covering up.

"But there's good stuff in their writings," she began, "full of principles. I love principles. I don't really want to give those books up. In fact, a lot of their writings have nothing to do with Mormonism, just principles and ethics! But," she sighed, "I'm anxious to be rid of this bewildering thing . . . so, okay. But," she added, "I don't see how saying words with my mouth will work when I don't feel like it inside."

"We'll say a prayer first," I said, taking her hand.

"But, I won't know what to say," she pleaded.

"That's okay. You just repeat after me." I began a simple prayer and Beth, sentence by sentence, dutifully repeated them. But when we came to where she was to say "I denounce the writings of Joseph Smith and Brigham Young," she startled all of us.

She rudely interrupted the prayer, refused to say it, and was ready to fight! "There's no way I can do that!" she said in irritation, her voice rising. "You don't know what profound and deep things they wrote! I haven't even read Christian books that have been that profound!"

I patiently waited while she vented her upset. Then she apologized. "I'm sorry—I'm determined to say it. Let's begin again."

I began the prayer again, and I could see her trying to subdue the turbulent feelings which threatened to erupt again. Sure enough, as I expected, when we came to the denouncement, the torrential flood broke loose and burst out of her mouth.

"I'm *not* going to do that—I can't!" Mad and angry, her arguing took on a more vehement tone. "It isn't going to work! How can it work, when inside I don't WANT to! You just don't know how *good* their writings *are*."

Again, I said quietly, "That's all right. Let's begin again."

We went through the prayer at least five times before she could bring herself to verbalize it—but amid much disputation and belligerence, she finally did: "In the name of Jesus," she said, "I denounce the writings of Joseph Smith and Brigham Young. But," she quickly added, "it's not going to work, because I don't *feel* like it! Nor do I *want* to!"

I smiled, "Beth, God's Word says that verbal confession is made unto salvation. You don't have to feel like it inside. You've confessed it with your mouth in the name of Jesus, and it will work."

She was emotionally drained. After we encouraged her by reading Scripture, she got up from her chair announcing that it was late and she had to go. As she left, she managed a weak smile. "I still don't see how it can work," she said.

Thirty minutes later, Judy and I also said our goodbyes. Pastor and Mrs. Smith promised to keep us posted.

Out in the car I told Judy, "You don't always do what I did tonight, unless you feel moved upon to do so. If it had been done too soon, or at the wrong time, it would probably have been the last time the Smiths would have seen Beth."

"Do you think she had a devil in her?" Judy asked.

"No," I said, "and this is where others and I part company. This is not to say that in some instances, especially with cults who are directly involved in satanic activities, that may not be so. But in the majority of cases, ex-cultists' problems usually stem from psychological enslavement. Beth just didn't want to give up something she loved. In her case, I'm sure what we did tonight will prove effective.

"While there are those who believe the only solution to an ex-cultist's emotional state is exorcism, I think it's because they don't understand what's happening to the individual. When they did it in my case, it was the ultimate humiliation. I was continually prayed over with commands that the 'Mormon devil' come out. It's a wonder I stayed. Some, sad to say, don't.

"I mention this because six months after I had accepted the

Lord, a Mormon lady attended one of our meetings. After the service a few of the ladies gathered around her and began praying for her. The Mormon lady bowed her head, obviously appreciating being prayed for. But the praying progressively became bolder and soon they were shouting, 'Come out, you Mormon devil!' I gasped and said to myself, 'Well, she won't be back.' And of course I was right—she never did. I could have told them it was the wrong thing to do, but their attitude was that I was only a baby Christian, so what could I possibly know? So, I kept quiet.

"If those who pray would simply change their wording to the effect that God would remove 'Mormon thinking' or the 'Mormon hold' or 'Mormon bondage' or have them renounce cult writings, it would probably prove just as effective.

Two weeks later I received a phone call from Pastor Smith. His wife was on the extension, and they were both excited.

"Someone wants to talk to you," they said. The next voice was Beth's.

"I don't know how it worked!" she began excitedly, "but it did! I went home that night thinking something that simple couldn't possibly work—especially since I didn't feel like it inside. But the next morning I awoke, and 'Mormonism' hadn't awakened me at any time during the night.

"I told myself it was just a coincidence. I decided I'd give it till noon, then if it didn't overpower my mind, I'd have to say it worked. Noon came, one week, two weeks went by, and it's gone! All I've been doing since is puzzling on how it worked. I'm really free of it! And all I did was say it!"

But freedom in one area doesn't mean there's freedom in another. It seems to come piecemeal. Pastor Smith told me later that even though Beth had said the sinners' prayer and was coming to church, she admitted that while she got rid of her Mormon books, she still had a problem giving up the *Book of Mormon* in her heart.

"Don't push it," I said. "That will come in time."

As I hung up the receiver, my thoughts drifted from our evening with Beth to my daughter, Linda. The *Book of Mormon* had also been a problem for her, and I learned that for each former cultist a different method might be used.

Linda and I were both attending Bible college. I recalled how surprised I was the day she told me what she did to break the final hold of Mormonism—more especially the *Book of Mormon.*

Prior to this day, she was always making discouraging statements: "Mom, I've been a Christian for three years now, and I've let go of all my Mormon doctrines. But if so, why am I continually in this state of turmoil, battling between Mormonism and Christianity? I'm so tired—why am I not totally free yet? What's left to do!"

I had no answer to give her. Saturday, she was gone all day. Then late afternoon she came into the house, her eyes red from crying. "Mom, God finally showed me what the problem was. And, He showed me what I had to do—and I did it!"

We sat down at the kitchen table, and she proceeded to tell me.

"The other night," she said, "God called my attention to the shelf in my closet. I looked, and there was my *Book of Mormon* which I had refused to discard when I became a Christian. To me it was the 'Word of God' as much as the Bible. I loved it, just as I loved God. Although believing Joseph Smith's *claim* about the book was false, I knew the *principles* in it were true—that what men like Nephi and Alma taught had to be true, as much as what Peter, John, and Paul taught.

"Then God started opening my mind. I began to see that by clinging to the book, principles or not, it kept me from becoming free and served to link me with the rest of Mormonism.

"But how was this to be undone? Then it came to me. I had to give the book up. But could I? That would be like giving up a part of God!

"After many hours of tears and struggle, I realized there was only one way I could finally be set free of Mormonism. I had to do something *to* that *Book of Mormon.*

"At first, I thought about giving it away or throwing it in the garbage, but those methods didn't seem satisfactory. Then God inspired me as to how. I was to verbally denounce it, then it would be out of my life. I also had to do away with it *literally.* I had to see it physically die—actually come to an end right in front of my own eyes. *I* must be the one to destroy it, and *I* must attend its funeral!

"With lots of tears and every ounce of strength and courage I could muster up, I took a spoon and a pack of matches and along with my *Book of Mormon* drove out of town to a secluded spot in the hills.

"I got out of my car, walked a short distance, then sat down in the dirt under some trees. After digging a good size hole in the ground, I began ripping out the pages of my precious *Book of Mormon* and placed them in the hole. I set the pages on fire and watched as they burned to ashes. Between my uncontrollable sobs, I forced myself to verbally denounce the *Book of Mormon* and all its teachings, even though at that moment I still loved it with all my heart.

"Devastated, I drove home, leaving what to me was 'God's Word' in ashes behind me. So here I am, and I don't know if it's going to work. I'll just have to wait and see."

A week later at breakfast, I asked her if she had noticed any change. She hesitated, then looked startled.

"Gosh, Mom! Do you know I haven't even thought about the *Book of Mormon* all week! Now that's a miracle! For the last three years I had a special room in my mind for the *Book of Mormon*. The slightest word could immediately open the door. But it's different now.

"Mom, I'm free! My mind and spirit are totally and one hundred percent *free!*" With that, she began to cry in gratitude and relief.

Another week later, I asked her the same question.

"Yes, Mom. It's like it's all been erased from that room in my mind—or like someone has taken a key and locked the door so I can't enter anymore. And, do you know, even when I try to, I can't! My thinking has been absolutely liberated from Mormonism. Oh Mom, no more confusion, no more battles—at last I'm really free!"

I shared Linda's experience with Pastor Smith and his wife. I suggested that when they sensed the timing was right, they could propose the same procedure to Beth if she was still having a problem with the *Book of Mormon*. "But," I explained, "Beth may come up with her own way—you may even hear of other methods through other pastors—I certainly don't have the last word on the subject. Just keep your ears and heart open to new ideas."

How Can Christians Help?

1. *Be conscious of the emotional state of the cultist.* Understand the fears and pressure the cult member is under and the courage it takes to contact a pastor. Acknowledge this to him or her.

2. *Do not take it personally if the cultist does not immediately relate to you.* Cultists view a Christian as very different from themselves. This is because they have been in a tightly knit group of those of like mind—they're not used to outsiders. One ex-cultist said, "When I contacted a pastor, I sensed he was a good man, but I felt like I was contacting an alien from another world. I was shaking the whole time I met with him."

3. *If the cultist is willing to meet with you in your home, do not pressure her to attend church, other than a gentle invitation.* If she is still active in her cult and investigating Christianity on the side, she will not want cult friends (spies) to find her out. Many will spend most of the time meeting with the pastor (or Christian friend) in a home rather than at church. Accept this.

4. *Do not rush the cultist into a commitment to Christ.* Even though a cult member has contacted you, he or she may not be ready. The logic that made him question his doctrines may have brought him to your door—but emotionally he's still tied to his cult.

5. *Be aware that some cultists who have already left their cult may not be seeking Christ.* They may only be seeking new relationships and a sense of belonging. This is because the question, "Who am I?" is answered in terms of "This is where I belong."

6. *Do not indulge in negative talk by blurting out where he is wrong and how wicked his cult is.* One ex-cultist said, "With my nerves so jangled, if the pastor had said one harsh word to me against Mormonism, he'd have lost me right then. I'd never have gone back!" Remind yourself of the story of the bank teller. When a teller is taught to know what a *genuine* bill feels and looks like, he can automatically detect a counterfeit. Give a cultist positive input about Christianity, and on their own he or she will automatically detect what's false about his or her own religion.

7. *Never relax your attentions by assuming the cultist's contact with you means he has given up his cult.* Although the cult member may be meeting with you, even attending your church, he is still analyzing whether he will fit in and whether Christian beliefs are compatible with his thinking. Unbeknown to you, he may even be investigating another cult on the side.

8. *At a point where you think he is ready, have the new believer denounce cult writings and cult leaders and rid his home of cult literature.* This, however, is not something that is to be done immediately. (I was only able to do this after I'd been a Christian a year.)

9. *Be prepared to give up your time.* When an ex-cultist is in the process of giving up securities, he or she will tend to revert to the parent-child role. The former cultist needs "mothering" or "fathering" and will thrive on it. The new believer will lean heavily on the pastor and his wife or whomever is working with him or her. There must be this intense attachment to someone for a period of time or the convert will become too fearful and insecure. The cultist's whole platform of beliefs or security blanket, so to speak, has been yanked from beneath him or her. Like a toddler the former cult member needs help in learning to walk all over again. During this critical time, the worker needs to supply the former cultist with decisive answers.

In addition, learn to be patient with the inevitable intrusion on one's time until the apron-strings are loosened and the new convert is able to transfer his or her dependency to Christ.

When the latter happens, the new believer may back off from the relationship. This is because it is too intense in light of his or her growing autonomy. Some counselors have been hurt, thinking something has happened to violate the relationship. Have they offended him? Is she planning to return to the cult? Not necessarily so. Like the adolescent who must eventually sever the umbilical cord, there will be a gradual pulling away from those who have been spiritually nurturing him or her.

10. *Communicate respect.* When a Mormon, for example, sincerely declares his belief in and love for Jesus Christ, one should show respect and resist the tendency to exhibit disbelief. An ex-Mormon, after being a Christian for thirteen years, said, "No

one can ever convince me that Jesus was not in my heart, for I love the same Jesus now that I did when a Mormon."

A Mormon, however, may have a long way to go to a fuller understanding of reconciliation and the Atonement, but this will come in due time. Even established Christians still grow in this understanding.

11. *When should a pastor allow an ex-cultist to be baptized?* Not everyone may agree, but I feel that it is not necessary to wait until the new convert has dropped every single cult belief. It will be extremely difficult for the former cultist to immediately rid himself of every cult concept (a fact the new convert may hide). Although it is a matter for the pastor to decide, consider the following testimony.

> I absolutely could not grasp my fallen or sin nature. I didn't even understand the sinner's prayer when I said it. As an ex-Mormon I believed that if I had committed no obvious act of sin, I shouldn't be classed as a sinner. If I did commit a sinful act, I believed it was the direct influence of the devil, certainly nothing to do with any Adam nature in me. After all, I was a child of God. Although my body might sin, my spirit was good. However, because I wasn't perfect, I knew there had been specific bad acts in my life, so I did understand repentance in that light. I knew Jesus died so I could repent of those sins.
>
> My first level of understanding of my Adamic nature was that the sin nature is simply in one's literal "skin" and "bones," because I kept hearing Christians talk about one's sinful "flesh." Once again, that had nothing to do with the real me, inside. I also knew Adam incurred a spiritual death and was cut off from the presence of God, but that was his sin, not mine.
>
> However, I wanted to be baptized because I loved Christ and wanted to serve Him. If I had been held back, waiting for a more correct understanding of the sin nature, I believe my growth in the church would have been seriously stunted. Baptism opened a door for me. After that, I began to comprehend more easily.
>
> I believe God's grace is bigger than most understand. God knew that for me the Adamic nature would be a gradual

realization, and He inspired my pastors to go ahead with my baptism. The Scripture says that with the lips confession unto salvation is made. It doesn't say, "with the mind's complete understanding salvation is made." Whatever level of understanding a Mormon is capable of should be accepted, and the revelation of the unfolding left to God and His timing.

Besides a cultist's decision to leave the cult, the first contact with a pastor is probably one of the bravest acts he or she will ever perform. One can only admire the cultist whose drive for truth is so strong that he or she is willing to subject themselves to the suffering and turmoil that results.

New converts face a difficult and rocky road for the first three years or longer. But they will come through it as long as there is a knowledgeable, caring, and understanding Christian by their side. Through this contact cult beliefs will eventually dissipate and be replaced with Christian beliefs—if they can maintain that contact long enough. Remember parents saying, "Don't hang around with the wrong crowd or you'll become one of them"—it also works with the right crowd.

Chapter 9 Notes

1. Eric Hoffer, in his book *The True Believer*, 114–115, explains that spying and suspicion surprisingly do not lead to dissension, but to "strict conformity" which, of course, the leaders want. He says that "fear of one's neighbors, one's friends and even one's relatives seems to be the rule within all mass movements."

2. Eileen Barker, "Defection from the Unification Church: Some Statistics and Distinctions," in *Falling from the Faith: Causes and Consequences of Religious Apostasy,* ed. David G. Bromley (Newbury Park, CA: Sage Publications), 172.

3. Dr. Margaret Singer, "Coming Out of the Cults," *Psychology Today* (January 1979): 80.

4. Latayne C. Scott, *Ex-Mormons: Why We Left* (Grand Rapids, MI: Baker Book House, 1990), 155–156.

10

THE PRECARIOUS
TRANSITION PERIOD

A time of critical analysis and special needs

I'm so excited." Judy said. "My problems are behind me, and now I'm looking forward to becoming a real part of my church!" But just as she was about to leap into her future, new problems began to arise—problems that Richard, Melanie, Myra, and Elizabeth also went through, each in their respective turns.

There is a danger period—that precarious stage after the new convert finally acknowledges cult beliefs as unbiblical, knows he or she made a correct decision in leaving, has pretty much dealt with the problems, and is just about to cross over the line into full assimilation into the Christian community.

It is at this point that former cultists suddenly find themselves entering an in-between stage. It is like crossing a bridge with the cult behind them at one end and the Christian community ahead—but they stop in the middle. In this suspended, limbo-like period, they are neither here nor there.

They are no longer firmly established in cult beliefs, but they are not yet firmly grounded in Christian beliefs. They no longer behave like an ex-cultist, but they do not yet behave like a Christian. They are between mores and beliefs. They are between two worlds, more especially, between two cultures.[1]

A "culture," says Philip R. Harris, "gives people a *sense* of who they are, of belonging, . . . how they should behave, and . . . what they should be doing."[2] And during this precarious in-between stage, this sense is entirely lost.

The new convert is suddenly aware that slipping away is a culture that defined who he or she was and what his or her role in life was. The new believer is losing the familiar world, signs, and symbols that had once been a part of his life space. Gone are personal convictions once held about God, the universe, and the meaning of one's place in it—everything that made life intelligible and meaningful. The fearful part is that the former cultist has not yet grown enough as a Christian to be convinced that life without these familiar symbols can prove as fulfilling.

He or she teeters on that middle line of demarcation, peering into an unknown future—wanting to retreat, to fall back into the arms of the cult with all its false securities. This does not mean the former cult member wants to embrace cult theology again. Nor does it mean he or she loves Jesus and Christianity less. It is because he senses what had at one time been so spiritually meaningful to him. However, he or she has come too far to turn around and go back. He has reached the point of no return.

This is where Judy found herself. Not only did she have to reconcile this crisis, but during this in-between stage she also had to face a period of intense self-analysis. While not all may experience this, she did. For some, contemplating one's new Christian identity instinctively requires reflecting upon the old. If done honestly, it can deal a crushing blow to the ego.

This was particularly hard on Judy. She had always prided herself on being autonomously intelligent and discerning. Now she had to take a second look at herself.

"This was a blow to me," she said. "Looking back over thirty years of Mormonism, I finally had to accept the stark truth that I did not have the intelligence to discern right from wrong. This raised some probing and painful questions: Could I ever trust myself again to make a correct choice? How did I know I was right about Christianity? Would I be fooled in this conversion like I was in the Mormon Church? How does one gauge truth?

"Having no answer to the last question and realizing that the strength and fervency of my former faith had not proved a reliable guide, I concluded I could no longer trust faith. I would, therefore, toss it from my life and operate solely on reason."

But for Judy this decision caused serious contradictions. "If I do this," she asked, "where does reason fit into spirituality? Isn't religion solely a faith matter? If I put reason first and faith last, will I somehow become an enemy to God?" Nevertheless, she proceeded with her resolve.

"I was determined," she said, "never to be duped again. Everything which claimed to be truth, including Christianity, would be subjected to verifiable facts and reason. If I confessed Christ, it would be from logic. If I believed in the Bible, it would be because it was a historical record. Doing it this way would bring me into safe harbor. Never again would I appear foolish by an incorrect decision concerning religion."

But in spite of her best intentions, a strange conflict raged. She was at war with something deep inside her which cried out for the exercise of faith. It warned her that if she relied on evidence and reason, faith would cease to exist—and this must not be!

Nevertheless, smothering the spiritual stirrings within her, she remained adamant. She would play it safe and never venture out in faith again. Still the battle persisted.

To overcome the conflict, she tried various tactics. "I forced myself," she explained, "to create a mental block that would make me incapable of perceiving anything in religion as sacred. That way faith could not rise up in my adoration of it.

"But it's crazy," she added. "I still found myself responding to the sacred anyway! For some reason my spirit *demanded* the exercise of faith. I also kept seeking a spirituality that required faith—faith, which I decided I must never again risk! I was so worn out I was ready to give up."

For Judy, the conflict was ruthless and unrelenting, the mental gymnastics strenuous and impossible. She had to tarry at that middle point of the bridge and work it through before she could move on. But she was no different than Richard, Melanie, Myra, and Elizabeth. They each stopped at the middle of the bridge, had their own period of self-analysis, their own adjustments to make, and their own set of questions that had to be answered before they could move on.

As the new convert moves forward from this point of the bridge, determined that Christianity will act as a substitute and fill one's life as effectively as the cult did, the new believer looks in the church to find his or her niche for fulfillment. But the former cultist soon meets disappointment. The rule of thumb that soon reveals itself is: *The greater the number of needs met in a cult, the greater the sense of loss in those churches that do not fill them.*

A former cultist, especially an ex-Mormon, used to having emotional, psychological, intellectual, and spiritual needs filled through intense cult programs, looks for the same highly stimulating opportunities in the church.

However, while traditional churches may provide fulfillment for spiritual and emotional needs, some often neglect the social and intellectual. Others, strictly acting as social communities, neglect the spiritual. A few believe the church should only address spiritual matters. One pastor's wife stated, "One shouldn't expect human needs to be met. It isn't spiritual!"

When dissatisfaction sets in, the new convert somehow knows his unrest has something to do with his former cult life but is unable to determine why. His statements, therefore, are ambiguous.

"My church just doesn't energize me like the Unification Church did!" Elizabeth moaned. "When I joined Reverend Moon, I really felt I'd found meaning and purpose to my life. To be honest, I haven't experienced that same kind of satisfaction in my new church."

Judy said, "Don't ask me why I don't feel fulfilled. It's just a kind of sense I have that something is missing in my life now, but it wasn't in the Mormon Church."

As soon as a former cultist discovers the answer, he or she

begins to harbor a secret nostalgia for the cult. At the same time, the new believer becomes critical of what his new church does *not* offer. Judy, Melanie, and Myra began to depreciate their respective churches.

"Why," Melanie asked, "if Christianity is God's only true church, hasn't the Holy Spirit inspired pastors to have church programs as perfect as the Mormon Church's?"

Myra essentially said the same: "If Christianity is true, you would think it would provide *more* than the cult."

All three recalled well-rounded Mormon programs. There were classes in world cultures, music, homemaking, scouting, parenthood, service projects, morality, work ethics, speech, literature, drama, self-improvement, goal-setting—all effectively designed for the spiritual, physical, moral, intellectual, and emotional growth of its members.

It was fortunate I had already gone through this stage—I knew what they were talking about.

While Judy, Melanie, and Myra did not voice their dissatisfactions to anyone outside our group—certainly not to Christian peers from whom they were seeking acceptance—I was bolder when it happened to me.

In frustration I asked my pastor, "Why don't you preach anything on ethics, morals, standards, integrity, industriousness, fine arts, education, the home, or self-improvement? Why teach only theological subjects and ignore subjects essential for the whole person? Why doesn't Christianity fill important needs like the Mormon Church does? Why are there so many voids?"

Like other ex-Mormons, I had a difficult time understanding that a Christian church has only one major objective—the preaching of the Gospel, not homemaking and English literature, subjects which I could obtain at any local college. It is not only a harsh shock after the wrenching disappointment of believing Christianity will be a substitute for the cult in all ways, but it delays assimilation into the church.

Myra declared, "I just have to keep reminding myself that just because a church isn't perfect doesn't mean it doesn't contain God's truth. But," she added, "it sure is difficult."

Another need the new convert hopes to fulfill is involvement in a strong cause.

Richard, extremely goal-oriented, said disappointedly, "I

observe Christians sitting in church, listening to sermons about Jesus, but what are they really doing? Where is their world-changing cause, their personal sacrifice? Aside from witnessing and some speaking against secular humanism in the public schools, they don't appear to have any."

Unconsciously, the new convert knows that causes supply purpose and meaning. But if she has entered a small church, there are only a few programs to become involved in and no avenues for intense commitment.

Linda also had something to say about it. "My church offers the youth high-idealed activities, special projects, even car washes to raise money because the leaders know group causes make young people 'tick.' But, they forget that adults also need to keep on 'ticking.'"

Does the average church claim world-changing causes? Hexham and Poewe note that whereas cults contend they are going to bring about a new social order, traditional religions appear to be incapable of this.[3] They point out that churches mainly have the reputation of offering solace to individuals in personal problems and relationship to God, but that's all.

Cults, on the other hand, do offer strong causes. Promising to change the world into a more idealistic community, they offer members meaning and purpose by promising they will become part of God's plan for a new world theocracy. Steve Hassan, author of *Combating Cult Mind Control,* says that considering present global concerns, one would have to be "stupid or apathetic to not want to hear what they have to say."[4]

But in the church the cause need not be social or political change. *Any* cause will do as long as it is God's, but it needs to be one in which the whole Christian community is involved. Unity is important to the ex-cultist. It's what he or she has been used to.

Since a former cultist has a lot to give, disappointment soon sets in when the church does not require as much as one is capable of giving. Maurice C. Burrell affirms this in his book *The Challenge of the Cults:* "Most orthodox Christians today pay lip-service to the ideal of an all-member ministry within the church. . . . many Christian congregations still rely heavily upon the clergyman or minister to further the church's real work and tend to use lay people only in matters concerned with things like bricks and mortar and finance. In contrast," he continues, "the sects take very seriously the full participation of every member in the life of the group. Each member is believed to have a significant part to play and, as a result, is made to feel important and wanted."[5]

When one comes from a cult that required total commitment to strong causes, entering a traditional church that does not demand the same is difficult to handle.

But, besides the lack of causes, there is another serious concern. The new convert looks for incentive programs to help him set personal goals. While personal goals can admittedly be set by oneself, former cultists are used to receiving them through specially designed programs and classes.

Melanie recalled the *Pursuit of Excellence* program, where girls under 18 were challenged with incentive awards.[6]

Judy remembered the womens' *Personal Progress Program* with nine areas for achievement: Developing Virtues of Womanhood, Spirituality, Service and Compassion, Homemaking, Health and Recreation, Cultural and Fine Arts, Education, Setting Goals, Personal and Social refinement.[7]

Richard also missed goal-setting. "After a year with the Hare Krishnas," he said, "you could acquire the title of Bhakti-Sastri, or ordained minister. Then you could enter the order of renouncement, called Sannyasa, and become a Svami."[8]

Men defecting from the Mormon Church recall advancement through three offices of the Aaronic Priesthood: Deacon, Teacher, and Priest, each with exclusive duties. Progressing to the Melchizedek Priesthood, there were the offices of Elder, Seventy, and High Priest. The "Law of Eternal Progression," a popular Mormon aphorism, was ever before the member with the challenge that there would never be an end to advancement or goal striving.

But why do members thrive on this? Vincent Herr, in *Religious Psychology*, says it provides an energy source for perseverance and acts as a "stabilizing mechanism." It keeps "the person stable and firm in the new direction which he has sought to maintain since he experienced conversion."[9]

This kind of satisfaction is, therefore, essential to happiness.

From the cult's perspective, the wisdom in providing this is that *a happy member becomes a committed member.* Those in our group who converted to a comparatively small church struggled with boredom, lack of direction, purposelessness, and insignificance. After a bustling life of cult activity and challenges, it was difficult to settle for only Sunday attendance. In addition, Judy, Melanie, and Myra believed it was the church's responsibility to provide for every human need they had.

Of course, this need for intense activity does not apply to the beginning of the ex-cultist's conversion. This quieter beginning time is for three reasons.

Some, after working themselves to the point of overload in the cult, desperately need a rest. Second, if they are bitter about the dedication they poured out in the cult and feel betrayed, they not only distrust themselves and others, but God. Third, many are so damaged, hurt, and disoriented that they are in no condition to desire anything else except salvation.

But, on the other hand, not every ex-cultist fits this mold. One's need to become involved and pursue challenges can take place within the first year. The new convert who has worked through initial problems and has arrived at that place on the bridge where activity is now important wants to serve! At that point, "the individual's most vital need," says Eric Hoffer in *The Ordeal of Change,* "is to prove his worth, and this usually means an insatiable hunger for action."[10]

To prove his worth adds an additional motive. If the new convert has an inferiority complex about being an ex-cultist, he feels that serving will make him more acceptable and prove he is valuable.

When a former cultist enters a church, he or she is much like the young adolescent struggling for acceptance by the right crowd. The new believer battles with the pain of wanting to receive recognition. In the cult he had an audience which appreciated, praised, and applauded as he performed and conformed. But with esteem no longer coming from cult peers, the new convert's hope is to achieve the same recognition by becoming a significant part of the church community.

Christians who feel this motive disqualifies him for service may say, "If the church tries to fill human needs, isn't this playing up to the individual's ego? Shouldn't the new convert bow, instead, to the feelings of worthlessness because somehow it is more godly?"

James C. Dobson lends an emphatic *no* to this. "It is my opinion, that great confusion has prevailed on this matter among followers of Christ. Some people actually believe that Christians should maintain an attitude of inferiority in order to avoid the pitfalls of self-sufficiency and haughtiness. I don't believe it . . . That teaching did not come from the Scriptures."[11]

What does the Bible say? Dr. Gary R. Collins, in his book *Can You Trust Psychology*, states, "The Bible does not condemn human potential. God's Word acknowledges, instead, that human beings have been created in the divine image, as finite replicas of God. We have dignity, value, and purpose. This is not because some humanistic psychology decides that people are valuable but because the God of the universe created us and declared that his creation was good. . . . He [God] does not demand that we then stamp out all ideas about the self and become passive, lackluster nonentities. On the contrary, He molds us into new creatures with reason for positive self-esteem because we are children of the King. He gives us spiritual gifts, abilities, and responsibilities that we can use to serve Christ, help others, and find genuine fulfillment in life."[12]

Dr. Lawrence J. Crabb Jr., in his book *Effective Biblical Counseling*, observes that self-actualization, which is the development of oneself into a "full, creative, self-expressing person," is "the ultimate and highest need in Maslow's system." It "comes close to the biblical concept of becoming mature in Christ, developing in ourselves those attributes which characterize the Lord and then expressing our God-given worth in freely worshiping God and in serving others by the exercise of our spiritual gifts."[13]

But, regardless of the motive, activity fills an important need for the new convert. It is all well and good to tell him that true significance comes from understanding who he is in Christ. But until he grows into that understanding, he needs to feel significant through service. Serving not only shows his devotion to God and publicly witnesses to others that he is happy in his new life, but also fulfills the five imperatives of identity, acceptance, approval, self-worth, and significance. Hoffer says that "action is, basically, a reaction against loss of balance—a flailing of the arms to regain one's balance."[14] Almost unconsciously, the new convert senses this.

Without this kind of insight, Dr. Crabb's thesis that "problems develop when the basic needs for significance and security are threatened," will prove valid.[15] Without it, counseling on a one-to-one basis will be unnecessarily prolonged. "Surely," as Collins notes, "the psychologist is right who stated that counseling between two isolated individuals is not nearly as effective as counseling that is backed up by church involvement."[16]

Judy and the others needed to serve despite the fact they still struggled with a few cult-related problems. They waited to be "called" to a position, expecting the procedure to be like the cult's. They soon discovered it was not.

"It took me a long time to find out," Melanie said, "that pastors don't call a member to a position as a result of receiving a revelation. One must volunteer and then be voted upon—and only after the board's methodical deliberation over one's gender as well as one's social and marital state." (This is only the case in some churches.)

Judy was shocked at this procedure. "In the Mormon Church you didn't have to volunteer for a position," she said. "Members were called to a position by their bishop who claimed direct revelation. This made you feel God Himself wanted to use you. Why can't pastors do the same? It makes me wonder if the clergy are really hearing from God!"

About a year after Linda's conversion, she telephoned me long distance, very distraught.

"Mom," she cried, "I thought serving in the church would be pleasing to God—that because He knows my heart, He'd see that I was called to some position!

"Remember how active we were in the Mormon Church, teaching classes and busy all the time? Contrary to what Christians believe, you know we didn't do it to earn heaven. We did it because we believed God would be happy with our faithfulness and dedication. Most of all, we wanted to serve Him!

"I've got to do something for God in my new church or else I'll go crazy! Doesn't God have a plan for my life other than salvation in general? Doesn't He want to utilize my talents? Am I of no value? I feel like I'm in a state of 'nothingness.' How can the Mormon Church be so outstanding and fulfilling in what it offers to its members and be wrong, and the Christian church be right and offer so little? Mom, did we make a mistake by leaving?"

Myra, too, eventually learned the procedure, but said it didn't work for her.

"I volunteered for a job—any job—," Myra related, "and found out the board's major consideration was whether I was still possessed by a 'cult devil' [an attitude not found in all churches]. How am I supposed to find purpose and meaning in an organization that devastates my self-image?"

Of course, when the new convert first enters the church, the former cultist is intelligent enough to know that one's problems are serious enough that even he or she would not expect to serve in any capacity. But some ex-cultists have discouragingly said that even after a long time, the hesitation still exists. Author Helen Ebaugh calls this the "hang over identity."[17] As Richard said, "Once an ex-cultist, always an ex-cultist."

"Even when I dropped hints," Richard continued, "I wasn't taken seriously. Even with outright volunteering, it never seemed to materialize." I've heard other ex-cultists say, "Try to let an ex-cultist volunteer for a church job and see how fast they're put to work."

However, in defense of churches, board members do have valid concerns—the new convert may still harbor cult beliefs. It would, of course, be out of the question to let a cultist of recent defection assume a leadership role like teaching. But it is, however, a serious mistake not to allow the new believer to contribute in some way.

For those churches which have reservations, the new convert's self-esteem sinks to a critical low. James Dobson says that self-esteem "is the most fragile characteristic in human nature, and once broken, its reconstruction is more difficult than repairing Humpty Dumpty."[18]

To avoid this crisis, some former cultists offer the following remedy: "After a year, when Christian doctrines are more firmly established, leave and transfer to another church unfamiliar with your cult background—and be sure to keep it a secret."

Richard did just that. Entering another church, he soon became involved. Since he was free of his cult at that point, he thought it unnecessary to tell his new pastor. After his credibility was established, he then told the pastor of his background. Switching churches proved effective for Richard and kept him from dropping out of the church.

Judy did the same. Eager to teach but having unknowingly entered a denomination which frowns on women teaching adult classes—especially single women—she also changed her church affiliation.

However, before one negatively labels ex-cultists as "church-hoppers," one must understand an important principle. *All behavior is motivated toward pursuing need-fulfillment.* Dr. Crabb emphasizes that every individual, whether one wants to admit it or not, is saying, "I need to feel significant, and I am motivated to somehow meet that need . . ."[19] Hoffer notes that "the most poignantly frustrated are those whose talents and temperament equip them ideally for a life of action but are condemned by circumstances to rust away in idleness."[20]

Ex-cultists do not want to become passive Christians. They want to contribute, to make a difference, and they'll do whatever it takes, even if it means changing churches. After having experienced a religious system where need-fulfillment was primary, new converts find that anything less is devastating.

Those who stay with their original church often find themselves lost in a world where they can no longer pour out their energies into commitment, dedication, love, mission, and purpose. They soon become bored, feel socially rejected, and secretly wish they were back in the cult where they were encouraged to serve. Some attempt an apathetic or stoic stance to keep from hurting, but this only leads to a diminishment of spirituality and eventual inactivity.

There is, however, one activity often asked of an ex-cultist during this period. It is public testimony against one's former cult. This is *not* what the ex-cultist needs.

He or she is asked for three reasons. First, others are eager to hear a new convert declare how terrible and satanic the cult was and how he was saved. Second, they believe it will be beneficial for the new convert. Third, they believe the new convert wants to. When asked for prematurely, the testimony often results in mixed emotions. Judy said, "My church thought I had as much disdain for the Mormon Church as they did. They assumed because I left the cult voluntarily that I'd be anxious to testify about its satanic nature . . . that I was elated about being delivered from such a wicked cult—the cult that meant so much to me—the cult that I loved!

"Although I no longer believed Mormon doctrine and could testify to that," she continued, "I wanted to testify to more. I wanted to enlighten them—by including the positive aspects of Mormon church-life. Established Christians seemed to be ignorant of the fact that cults do have this side to them. But, of course, I knew better."

Judy admitted that like many others, she complied by responding with the usual happy facade. "How would it have looked if I had said no?" she said. "I agreed because I interpreted it as a rite of passage.

"However," she continued, "the performance of this rite led me to incorporate negative statements about the Mormon Church that only had one aim—Christian approval. I felt I had to convince everyone, myself as well, that I belonged. I felt that to pass this test, I had to declare their same stance against Mormonism so I could be classified as 'one of them.' It was not an authentic testimony."

Judy's example does not mean, however, that there are not those who testify because they are genuinely ready to do so. For those who are and find themselves in demand by various organizations, it gives them a busy life and sense of cause. But since it takes anywhere from three to eight years to work through cult-related problems, many are asked prematurely.

The kind of involvement a new believer seeks is a service position—to feel one is an integral part of the functioning body. If a new convert is unable to resume the same industrious kind of life-style she had in the cult, she will develop varying behavioral problems—among them, retreat. She will either "church-hop" to find satisfaction in another church, drop out, or return to the cult where she knows she will feel secure and be encouraged to serve.

If, however, the new convert has reached the point of no return and cannot go back to the cult, she may decide to retire totally from the religious scene. If she does this, the spiritual results are comparable to what often happens to early retirees from secular jobs. They die! They die a kind of mental, emotional, and spiritual death due to the slowdown of self-actualizing opportunities.

On the other hand, being allowed to serve will supply meaning to the new believer's life. It will reinforce his or her new identity and provide acceptance by the church community. "Man," stated Earl Biddle, "is not an unfeeling automaton, and all efforts to make him a soulless cog in a machine are destined to failure."[21]

How Can Christians Help?

1. *Practice a non-judgmental stance.* In the midst of the up-and-down swings typical of an ex-cultist, it is important that the new believer feels he can share with whomever is working with him. To assure this, provide a noncritical environment which will allow the former cultist to discuss problems without fear of judgment.

2. *Define the "in-between stage" to the new convert.* It may be difficult to determine when a new believer has reached that precarious in-between stage, especially if anxieties are covered up. But if the former cultist begins to exhibit problematic behavior similar to when he first defected, it is probably an indication. However, he may not understand what is happening.

Explain that this stage is the moment when he suddenly realizes that his former beliefs and securities are slipping away from him—for good. He is leaving the security of one world and moving toward another that is less familiar. Assure him the stage is normal and his feeling of being between two worlds is his own psychological condition, not a perspective of how other Christians perceive him. His acceptance of Christ made him a member of the family of God, and he now has equal status in the church community.

3. *At the middle of the bridge is there the chance the new convert could return to the cult?* Yes. It is a time of questioning and

searching and a time where he feels he doesn't belong anywhere. Lack of service opportunities may translate into nonacceptance. This makes him feel worthless. Proverbs 18:14 asks, "A wounded spirit who can bear?" When a person feels this way, says Crabb, "he will make it a top priority matter to protect himself from an increase in those unbearable feelings . . ."[22] How will an ex-cultist protect himself? By dropping out or returning to the cult.

4. *For the convert on the bridge who questions his judgment in faith matters and wonders how to measure truth, use the following analogy:*
If two people are arguing over the true measurements of an object, such as a length of plywood, they must resort to finding a standard or scale set by secular law which will provide accurate measuring. Thus, they use a ruler and arrive at what the truth is about the plywood's measurements.

Measuring spiritual truth works the same way. One needs to look for a standard but, in this instance, one set by spiritual law. The Bible is the standard. Within its pages are the guidelines for accurately measuring truth.

Remind the ex-cultist that the standard is not based on feeling, fervency of faith, or the ability to make a choice by reason. It is the Bible. God's Word alone is designed to prevent individuals from being tossed to and fro by every wind of doctrine.

5. *Explain to the former cultist what to expect in his or her church.* Some ex-cultists are "spoiled" in what to expect from their new church. A new convert may come from a cult which offered extensive need-fulfilling programs. The Mormon Church, for example, deliberately incorporates secular subjects into their theology, recognizing that it will satisfy members so they won't be tempted to look elsewhere. The former Mormon will expect his or her new church to provide something comparable. It is, therefore, important that the local church be defined so he knows what to expect. Do not let the new convert continue in disappointment after disappointment.

Linda described her dilemma when she first converted: "I was used to having all my cultural and academic needs met in the Mormon Church. It spoiled me by providing everything.

After I came into a Christian church and realized the voids, I kept saying to myself, 'Well, this is it. I'll just have to stay and be satisfied—somehow.'" Then, she added, "But I felt that if God was concerned about every bit of me as a human being, it seemed he would see to it that I was fulfilled through the church. I know Christians say that just worshiping Jesus and reading the Bible is all you need, but they need to wake up and smell the coffee! Jesus is supposed to enter all other facets and interests of a person's life, too. And, if so, these should be accessible through church. Sure, I eventually learned that I would have to take outside classes in science or the arts, but at the time I felt secular subjects should be incorporated within the church so there could be a Christian perspective applied."

If the new convert's church does not provide classes such as these, the former cult member needs to know it. He or she also needs to be told that it is up to the individual to seek out other avenues like college classes which can provide for his or her intellectual, emotional, and psychological needs—in other words, to pursue whatever subjects the church does not supply.

Although Linda gradually recognized that the spiritual growth she gained through fellowship at church, listening to sermons, and reading the Bible enabled her to carry her Christian perspective with her outside the church, she said, "It absolutely *never* dawned on me that I had to assume this responsibility myself. I really thought it was up to the church to supply all of this for me."

When I asked if she felt it would be interpreted as negative for a Christian to tell her the church was unable to fulfill such a wide range of needs, her reply was, "No. These are just the facts—the way things are," she said, "and it should be stated."

6. *If the new convert becomes strangely unhappy, what can be done?* His state may be because he feels purposeless. The most effective tool against this is to make him feel useful through some service in the church.

However, this must not be pushed on the ex-cultist. Each individual is different. While an ex-Mormon may look forward to involvement, an ex-Moonie may not. However, after some time all ex-cultists should be offered jobs, if possible, because activity keeps one in the church and strengthens faith.

Since it is understood that one would not place an ex-cultist in a place of spiritual leadership while he is still a novice, a survey of various denominations suggests positions pastors feel safe in letting an ex-cultist fill.

- involvement in a support group
- home Bible study, preparing coffee, refreshments
- working in the caring ministries such as cards to the ill and shut-ins; aiding the homeless, hungry, and transients; visiting nursing homes
- team teaching
- ushering
- helping in Children's Church, aiding in children's crafts
- committee work such as mission committee, prayer committee, or finance committee
- maintaining physical properties of the congregation, janitorial set-up and tear-down assistance
- office help such as photocopying, folding, preparing mailings, filing
- choir
- parking lot attendant, door greeter, distributing Sunday bulletins

Those pastors who had experience with ex-cultists commented that they were excellent workers. One even said he appreciated the new insights they brought into the church. Those churches which provided these opportunities also felt that placing new converts in positions eliminated any feelings of discrimination.

Former cultists, like everyone else in this world, need sanction, significance, value, love, and identity. They must feel total acceptance in their church and be given opportunities for service. This will not only fulfill their desire to serve God but also establish their identity in the church community, confirm their self-worth, and fulfill God-implanted needs.

A church must not only ask itself if it has succeeded in drawing the former cultist closer to God or whether it has convinced him of his cult's error. It must also ask, "Is the former cultist allowed to fulfill needs which are surfacing as a by-product of becoming newly committed to Christ and the church?" [23]

Richard, Myra, Melanie, Judy, and Elizabeth had a rough

time, not only during their time on the bridge but after they stepped across the line. But they made it. I was thankful God let me witness the transformation that took place in their lives. It confirmed Philippians 1:6 and John 8:32 to me—that God is faithful and will finish the work He starts and that knowing the truth does indeed set one free!

Chapter 10 Notes

1. Susan Rothbaum, "Between Two Worlds: Issues of Separation and Identity After Leaving a Religious Community," in *Falling From the Faith: Causes and Consequences of Religious Apostasy*, ed. David G. Bromley (Newbury Park, CA: Sage Publications, 1988), 205ff.

2 Philip R. Harris and Robert T. Moran, *Managing Cultural Differences* (Houston: Gulf Publishing Co., 1987), 12.

3. Irving Hexham and Karla Poewe, *Understanding Cults and New Religions* (Grand Rapids, MI: Eerdmans Pub. Co., 1987), 125–126.

4. "Mind Control Expert Sees Cult Growth" *Fellowship Today* (Coram, NY: August 1991): 8 .

5. Maurice C. Burrell, *The Challenge of the Cults* (Grand Rapids, MI: Baker Book House, 1984), 154–155.

6. *Pursuit of Excellence* (Salt Lake City: The Church of Jesus Christ of Latter-day Saints, 1978).

7. *My Personal Progress* (Salt Lake City: The Church of Jesus Christ of Latter-day Saints, 1983), 1–62.

8. Walter Martin, *The New Cults* (Ventura, CA: Vision House, 1983), 91.

9. Vincent V. Herr, *Religious Psychology* (Staten Island, NY: St. Paul Publications, Alba House, 1965), 119–120.

10. Eric Hoffer, *The Ordeal of Change* (New York: Harper & Row, 1963), 30. Used with permission of HarperCollins Publishers.

11. James C. Dobson *Hide or Seek* (Old Tappan, NJ: Fleming H. Revell Co., 1979), 184.

12. Gary R. Collins, *Can You Trust Psychology? Exposing the Facts and Fictions* (Downers Grove, IL: InterVarsity Press, 1988), 145.

13. Lawrence J. Crabb Jr., *Effective Biblical Counseling: A Model for Helping Caring Christians Become Capable Counselors* (Grand Rapids, MI: Zondervan, 1977), 79-80. Used with permission of Zondervan Publishing House.

14. Hoffer, 32.

15. Crabb, 69.

16. Collins, 23.
17. Helen Rose Fuchs Ebaugh, "Leaving Catholic Convents: Toward a Theory of Disengagement," David G. Bromley, op cit., 114.
18. Dobson, 62.
19. Crabb, 77.
20. Eric Hoffer, *The True Believer* (A Mentor Book, The New American Library, 4th printing, May 1962), 112. Used with permission of HarperCollins Publishers.
21. W. Earl Biddle, *Integration of Religion and Psychiatry* (New York: Macmillan Co., 1955), 88.
22. Crabb, 68.
23. Maurice C. Burrell's *The Challenge of the Cults* (Grand Rapids: Baker Book House, 1984, 151ff. Enumerates other lessons and challenges churches can learn from the cults if they hope to compete.

EPILOGUE

This book has presented very candidly the feelings and concerns of defectors from a cult. While every ex-cultist is an individual and one may suffer more or less than another, they do share common problems.

The Christian worker should not be overwhelmed at the task. Since God led the cultist out, He will finish the work He started—as long as there is a dedicated Christian willing to be there for the ex-cultist and go the extra mile.

That "mile" consists of gathering as much information about the ex-cultist and his former world as possible and, more especially, acquiring needed empathy. If workers neglect to understand all details of an ex-cultist's former culture and what he is going through, they will fail to establish necessary rapport.

Another part of that "mile" is sensitivity to the ex-cultist's feelings about self-worth. Christians, anxious to convert cultists, do not intentionally mean to put them down. But when new believers hear offensive statements against the religious culture they once loved, they are further robbed of self-esteem.

Some may say, "We are only denouncing the cult, not the individual." But often the ex-cultist cannot make that distinction. In addition, he or she not only decides this kind of degrading attack is not representative of Christ's love, but depression and a feeling of worthlessness set in that is serious enough to hinder one's progression in Christ. For the new convert to work through his or her anxieties, personal worth and self-esteem are critical.

A study on self-esteem, conducted by New York State University, revealed that individuals with low self-esteem will not persevere in solving difficult problems. Those who have high self-esteem will. This means that the ex-cultist who is divested of self-esteem will give up trying to work through his or her problems. The one who hasn't lost this quality will persevere.

Contributing further to the diminishment of self-worth is being classified as a "baby Christian," an unfortunate term. Because of this, the former cultist feels he is not taken seriously—that his judgment about certain matters is invalid. This is especially felt when trying to talk about his former cult life.

For myself, I was anxious to share some of my cult experiences because those events convinced me God was watching over me. I thought my new Christian friends would enjoy hearing about them—that they would be faith-promoting. But when I tried, I was always met with reserved stares. I kept saying to myself, *Why can't Christians understand that I had some great experiences in the Mormon Church, independent of its doctrines?* (Thirteen years later, I still cherish those experiences.)

In addition, when former cultists try to explain that within the cult, members actually had a genuine love for each other and describe, as Dr. Singer notes, the "warm friendships . . . the sense that group living taught them to connect more openly and warmly to other people than they could before their cult days"[1]—all one receives are looks of pity.

Myra also became disheartened over this. "Why," she asked, "do Christians think good experiences aren't possible for a cultist? Sometimes Christians make statements about life in the Mormon Church that I know are just not so. Why aren't they honestly interested in finding out what life is like within a cult? More than once I was told, 'God doesn't hear or answer a cultist's prayers.' There is no way I'll ever believe that! How do they think I was led out? Because God heard and answered this cultist's prayer!"

Judy was also saddened because no one believed that as a Mormon she had a heart after God. "I felt sad and hurt when Christians who worked with me assumed I wasn't acquainted with the Jesus of the Bible—or that I didn't believe He died for my sins. Gradually it made me withdraw from talking with them about it. I loved Jesus while I was in the Mormon Church. They didn't seem to understand that my whole prayer life and devotion was consecrated, not to the Mormon concept of God, but to the God I personally believed in—the same one I believe in today as a Christian."

After listening to Judy express her love for the biblical God and her gratitude for what Jesus did on the cross, I decided it couldn't be questioned. Like many cultists, she was introduced to the Bible during childhood and entered a cult hoping to further her love and service for God. She was no different than many others.

This often raises the question, Are there some saved cultists? John Allen, in *Shopping For a God,* offers his viewpoint:

> Again, there are without doubt many real Christians—confused, perhaps, and in an inconsistent position, but nonetheless Christians—within the fold of cult groups. Irving Hexham and Myrtle Langley testified after close study of the Unification Church, "It must be stated that we have met some individual Moonies who were very definitely Christians and others who have been truly converted to Christ through the Unification Church." [Allen continues] So have I; so have most Christian workers who have had much to do with the movement.[2]

Everyone has a time and a season, and when it's time for those in the above "inconsistent position" to come out, God makes it happen. However, in spite of this, ex-cultists still have a difficult time. Besides undoing many beliefs, there is the strain of covering up problems, suffering from stress-related ailments, striving for Christian acceptance, trying to conform, frustration (in some churches) over not being put to work, social crisis due to an inferiority complex, pressure to give up cherished beliefs too fast, and the overall wearing down under the emotional pain of not understanding what is happening and feeling no one else does either.

It is essential that a defector's new move into a traditional church offer a secure religious experience that will alleviate all anxieties and fulfill human imperatives. When this does not happen, repercussions are inevitable and new believers will be more difficult to work with.

Christians, hesitating to enter the ring with a defector because they're unfamiliar with professional counseling techniques, need not hold back. All that is required is teaching the former cultist basic Bible concepts, helping him with the principles of confession, renouncing, putting on the spiritual armor, and assuring him that Christ's power will enable him or her to get through this ordeal. In addition, empathy, caring, being available over the long haul to strengthen "feeble arms and weak knees," and a willingness to share the burden is enough.

When one can relay the following to the former cultist, it will make all the difference in the world: "I know it's tough, and I recognize that you have serious problems. I know you have given up something you loved very dearly and that you feel no one understands. But I want you to know that I'm here for you, to share your burdens in confidence, and we'll see it through together."

The new believer's reaction at that point will probably be similar to Dr. Dobson's portrayal of the problematic individual when, after believing himself to be alone in his difficulties, suddenly receives support:

> Someone cares! Someone understands! Someone assures me with professional confidence that he is certain I will survive. I'm not going to drown in this sea of despondency, as I feared. I have been thrown a life preserver by a friend who promises not to abandon me in the storm.[3]

The Christian who can act as that lifeline, establish genuine

communication through cultural sensitivity, and show unconditional love will establish a rapport that will see the former
cultist through to full spiritual maturity.

Epilogue Notes

1. Margaret Singer, "Coming Out of the Cults," *Psychology Today* (January 1979): 80.
2. John Allen, *Shopping For a God: Fringe Religions Today* (Grand Rapids: Baker Book House, 1987), 194-195. Hexham's quote is from "Cracking the Moonie Code," CRUX Vol. XV No. 3, September 1979, 27.
3. James C. Dobson, *Hide or Seek* (Old Tappan, NJ: Fleming H. Revell, 1979), 146.

APPENDIX

Witnessing Aids

Cetnar, Bill. "How to Witness to a Jehovah's Witness." Audio cassette tape. Available through Personal Freedom Outreach, P.O. Box 26062, Saint Louis, MO 63136. (Lecture by former high-ranking Jehovah's Witness.)

"Cults Bibliography." Pamphlet listing available publications. Available from Christian Research Institute International, P.O. Box 500, San Juan Capistrano, CA 92693.

Decker, Ed. "Some Pointers on Witnessing to Your Mormon Friends." Pamphlet. Available through Saints Alive in Jesus, P.O. Box 1076, Issaquah, WA 98027.

"Divine Truths in the Book of Mormon." Witnessing tract concerning contradiction between the Book of

Mormon and current Mormon theology. Available through Personal Freedom Outreach, P.O. Box 26062, Saint Louis, MO 63136.

Enroth, Ronald M. (ed.) *Evangelizing the Cults.* Ann Arbor, MI: Servant Publications, n.d.

Gardner, Jim and Cindy. "Jim and Cindy Gardner: 'classic Mormons' . . . discover Jesus!" Audio tape. (To share with Mormons.) Available through Saints Alive in Jesus, P. O. Box 1076, Issaguah, WA 98027.

Lewis, Gordon R. *Confronting the Cults.* Grand Rapids, MI: Baker Book House, 1966.

Lingle, Wilbur. "Witnessing Effectively to the Jehovah's Witnesses" Tape #12. Available through Personal Freedom Outreach, P.O. Box 26062, Saint Louis, MO 63136.

MacGregor, Lorri. *What You Need to Know About Jehovah's Witnesses.* Eugene, OR: Harvest House, 1992. Available through Saints Alive in Jesus, P.O. Box 1076, Issaquah, WA 98027.

MacGregor, Lorrie. "The Witness at Your Door," by ex-Jehovah's Witness. Video. Available through Saints Alive in Jesus, P.O. Box 1076, Issaquah, WA 98027.

Martin, Paul R. "Dispelling the Myths: The Psychological Consequences of Cultic Involvement." *Christian Research Journal.* 1989, Winter/Spring, 9-14. Available through Christian Research Institute International, P.O. Box 500, San Juan Capistrano, CA 92693. Also Wellspring Retreat & Resource Center, P.O. Box 67, Albany, OH 45710. (The latter is a rehabilitation and counseling program for persons emerging from totalist/cult experiences.)

Martin, Walter. "The Do's and Don'ts of Witnessing to the Cults." *Cults Reference Bible.* Available through Christian Research Institute International, P.O. Box 500, San Juan Capistrano, CA 92693.

McKeever, Bill. "Answering Mormons' Questions." (Minneapolis, MN: Bethany House Pub, 1991). Available through Utah Missions, Inc., P.O. Box 348, Marlow, OK 73055.

Passantino, Robert and Gretchen. *Answers to the Cultist at Your Door.* Eugene, OR: Harvest House Publishers, 1981.

"The Plain Truth of Herbert W. Armstrong." Witnessing tract for members of Worldwide Church of God, examining its history and major doctrines. Available through Personal Freedom Outreach, P.O. Box 26062, Saint Louis, MO 63136.

"Reaching the Cults for Christ." Article. Available through Christian Research Institute International, P.O. Box 500, San Juan Capistrano, CA 92693.

"Sharing Christ with Mormons." Audio tape. Available through Saints Alive in Jesus, P.O. Box 1076, Issaquah, WA 98027.

Smith, John L. "How to Witness to Mormons." Cassette tape. Available through Utah Missions, Inc., P.O. Box 348, Marlow, OK 73055.

Smith, John L. "Witnessing Effectively to Mormons." (Marlow, OK: Utah Missions, Inc., 1991.) Booklet available through Utah Missions, Inc., P.O. Box 348, Marlow, OK 73055.

Spencer, Jim. *Have you Witnessed to a Mormon Lately?* Vienna, VA: Chosen Books, 1986. Available through Saints Alive in Jesus, P.O. Box 1076, Issaquah, WA 98027.

Spencer, Jim. "Witnessing to Mormons." Video; also in audio tape. Available through Saints Alive in Jesus, P.O. Box 1076, Issaquah, WA 98027.

"Suggestions for Witnessing to Mormons." Witnessing tract. Available through Personal Freedom Outreach, P.O. Box 26062, Saint Louis, MO 63136.

Sundholm, Conrad and Sandra. "Witnessing and the LDS Mindset." Seminar tape package. Available through Saints Alive in Jesus, P.O. Box 1076, Issaquah, WA 98027.

Tanner, Jerald. *Problems in Winning Mormons* (Utah Lighthouse Ministry.) Available through Utah Lighthouse Ministry, P.O. Box 1884, Salt Lake City, UT 84110.

"A True Christian Presentation to a Jehovah's Witness." Witnessing tract. Available through Personal Freedom Outreach, P.O. Box 26062, Saint Louis, MO 63136.

"The Unification Church: The Christian View." Slides and cassette. Filmstrip version also available through Personal Freedom Outreach, P.O. Box 26062, Saint Louis, MO 63136. (Examines history, doctrines, indoctrination methods. Witnessing suggestions included in closing segment.)

"The Way of Private Interpretation." Witnessing tract for members of The Way International. Available through Personal Freedom Outreach, P.O. Box 26062, Saint Louis, MO63136.

"Who's That Knocking At Your Door?" Pamphlet on Mormons. Available through Saints Alive in Jesus, P.O. Box 1076, Issaquah, WA 98027.

"Witnessing Tips—A Jesus Style of Evangelism." Article. Available through Christian Research Institute International, P.O. Box 500, San Juan Capistrano, CA 92693.

"Witnessing to Cultists." Pamphlet. Christian Research Institute International, P.O. Box 500, San Juan Capistrano, CA 92693.

"Witnessing to Mormons." Video. Available through Utah Missions, Inc., P.O. Box 348, Marlow, OK 73055.

"Witnessing to Your Mormon Friends." Tract. Available through Saints Alive in Jesus, P.O. Box 1076, Issaquah, WA 98027.

Other Books:

"The Aftermath of Victimization: Rebuilding Shattered Assumptions," Ronnie Janoff-Bulman. *Trauma and Its Wake: The Study and Treatment of Post-Traumatic Stress Disorder.* (ed.) Charles R. Figley, Ph.D. New York: Bunner/Mazel Publishers, 1985.

Andres, Rachel and James R. Lane (ed.). *Cults and Consequences.* Jewish Federation Council. Available through

Cult Awareness Network, 2421 W. Pratt Blvd., Suite 1173, Chicago, IL 60645. (Help for understanding cults.)

Brandon, N. *The Psychology of Self-esteem*. New York: Bantam Books, 1969.

Braun, Bennett, M.D. (ed.) *Treatment of Multiple Personality Disorder*. American Psychiatric Press. Available through Cult Awareness Network, 2421 W. Pratt Blvd., Suite 1173, Chicago, IL 60645. (Particularly insightful for those who work with ritual abuse victims or victims of torture.)

Burrell, Maurice C. *The Challenge of the Cults*. Grand Rapids, MI: Baker Book House, 1981.

Carlson, Ron. "Understanding Mormonism." Audio tape. (Presents a compassionate case.) Available through Saints Alive in Jesus, P.O. Box 1076, Issaquah, WA 98027.

"Cults," Journal of the American Medical Association, 242, 3:279-80.

Enroth, Ronald. *Recovering from Churches that Abuse*. Grand Rapids, MI: Zondervan, 1994.

Ford, Wendy. *Recovery From Abuse Groups*. n.p., n.d. Available through American Family Foundation, P.O. Box 2265, Bonita Springs, FL 33959.

Ford, Wendy. *Some Thoughts on Recovery*. Available through CAN (Cult Awareness Network), 2421 W. Pratt Blvd., Suite 1173, Chicago, IL 60645.

Giambalvo, Carol. *Exit Counseling: A Family Intervention*. Bonita Springs, FL: American Family Foundation. Available through American Family Foundation, P.O. Box 2265, Bonita Springs, FL 33959. (Dispels myths of magical solutions in counseling and covers exit counseling.)

Goldberg, Lorna and William Goldberg, "Group Work with Former Cultists." *Social Work*, 27 (March 1982).

Hamilton, V. and D. Warburton (ed.). "Psychological Response to Serious Life Events." *Human Stress and Cognition*, New York: Wiley, 1980.

Hassan, Steven. *Combatting Cult Mind Control.* Rochester, VT: Park Street Press, 1988. (Inside view of cult life with view of deep psychological disturbances and personality changes that it can cause.)

Langone, Michael, (ed.). *Recovery from Cults: Help for Victims of Psychological and Spiritual Abuse.* New York: W. W. Norton & Co., 1993. Available through American Family Foundation, P.O. Box 2265, Bonita Springs, FL 33959.

Magnani, Duane. *A Problem of Communication.* Clayton, CA: Witness, Inc., 1989. Available through Witness, Inc., P. O. Box 597, Clayton, CA 94517.

Martin, Paul, *Cult-Proofing Your Kids.* Grand Rapids, MI.: Zondervan, 1993 (Advice on educating family members on cults. Last chapter is on how to help your child recover from cult involvement.)

Ross, Joan and Dr. Michael D. Langone. *Cults: What Parents Should Know.* American Family Foundation, Lyle Stuart Books, 1988. Available through American Family Foundation, P.O. Box 2265, Bonita Springs, FL 33959. (Practical guidelines for families and others seeking to help cultists or ex-cultists. Includes improving communications and rapport.)

Singer, Margaret Thaler, *Cults, Coercion, and Society.* Available through CAN (Cult Awareness Network), 2421 W. Pratt Blvd., Suite 1173, Chicago, IL 60645. (Reviews problems cults pose to society and the damage they inflict upon individuals.)

Stoner, Carroll and Cynthia Kisser. *Touchstones: Reconnecting After a Cult Experience.* Available through CAN (Cult Awareness Network), 2421 W. Pratt Blvd., Suite 1173, Chicago, IL 60645. (Covers process of separation from a cult, what made them leave, and how they managed their recovery and restructured their lives.)

Sullivan, Lawrence Bennett, "Counseling and Involvement in New Religious Groups." *Cultic Studies,* Journal 1 Fall/Winter 1984: 178-95.

Tanner, Jerald and Sandra, *Mormonism—Shadow or Reality?* Salt Lake City, UT: Utah Lighthouse Ministry, 1987). Available through Utah Lighthouse Ministry, P.O. Box 1884, Salt Lake City, UT 84110.

Tobias, Madeleine and Janja Lalich. *Captive Hearts, Captive Minds.* Claremont, CA: Hunter House, n.d. Available through American Family Foundation, P.O. Box 2265, Bonita Springs, FL 33959. (Addresses post-cult recovery issues.)

Resource Organizations

Many of the following organizations have newsletters with articles pertinent to cults, tips on witnessing, and other literature too lengthy to list. You may contact them at the following addresses:

American Family Foundation, P.O. Box 2265, Bonita Springs, FL 33959.

Answers In Action, P. O. Box 2067, Costa Mesa, CA 92628.

Christian Research Institute International, P.O. Box 500, San Juan Capistrano, CA 92693.

Cult Awareness Network (CAN), 2421 W. Pratt Blvd., Suite 1173, Chicago, IL 60645.

International Cult Education Program, P.O. Box 1232, Gracie Station, New York, NY 10028. (Focuses on preventive strategies, including young people exposed to cults on school campuses.)

Personal Freedom Outreach, P.O. Box 26062, Saint Louis, Missouri 63136. (Many tracts, tapes, and cassettes available, as well as Newsletter.)

Saints Alive in Jesus, P.O. Box 1076, Issaquah, WA 98027.

Spiritual Counterfeits Project, P.O. Box 4308, Berkeley, CA 94704.

Through the Maze Ministries, P.O. Box 3804, Idaho Falls, ID 83403. (Mormon material.)

Utah Lighthouse Ministry, P.O. Box 1884, Salt Lake City, Utah 84110.

Watchman Fellowship, Inc., P.O. Box 19416, Birmingham, AL 35219. (Publishes the "Expositor," a monthly newsletter with witnessing tips to cultists.)

Wellspring Retreat & Resource Center, P.O. Box 67, Albany, OH 45710.

Witness, Inc., P.O. Box 597, Clayton, CA 94517.

ABOUT THE AUTHOR

During the latter part of Janis Hutchinson's thirty-six years in the Mormon Church, she joined the underground system of Mormon fundamentalism, a movement that strives to maintain the original teachings of Mormonism. While participating in this underground movement, she was caught secretly attending a Christian church.

Accused of worshipping at the "altar of Baal," she was held against her will for several months and pressured to repent and renounce the Christian Jesus. She refused and nearly lost her life in the process. With God's help, she escaped and later received Christ.

Janis is deeply committed to helping established Christians acquire understanding and sensitivity to the problems of former cult members, which often persist for three to eight years after they come to Christ. Her desire is to aid Christians in grasping the full extent of their witnessing responsibility.

Janis Hutchinson is available to speak at weekend retreats, women's groups, church services, conferences, and other gatherings.

If you wish to correspond with the author, please write to her at:

Janis Hutchinson
P.O. Box 374
Everett, WA 98206

If you would like more information about the author's speaking schedule and topics, please call:

Carol Christensen

1-206-776-6097